E-Teaching

Creating Web Sites and
Student Web Portfolios
Using Microsoft PowerPoint®

Jay D'Ambrosio, M.A.

Linworth
PUBLISHING, INC

Library of Congress Cataloging-in-Publication Data

D'Ambrosio, Jay.
  E-teaching : creating Web sites and student Web portfolios using
Microsoft Powerpoint / by Jay D'Ambrosio.
       p. cm.
Includes bibliographical references and index.
  ISBN 1-58683-129-1 (pbk.)
  1. Web sites--Design--Study and teaching. 2. Microsoft PowerPoint
(Computer file) 3. Internet in education. 4. Portfolios in education.
I. Title.
  TK5105.888.D355 2003
  005.7'2--dc22
                              2003016549

Published by Linworth Publishing, Inc.
480 East Wilson Bridge Road, Suite L
Worthington, Ohio 43085

ISBN: 1-58683-129-1

5 4 3 2

Table of Contents

Table of Figures

Acknowledgments

I would like to thank the following individuals for their tireless dedication to making this book a reality:

- Louis A. Nagy, Ed.D. for his guidance and suggestions throughout the development of this work
- Greg Hayward, Tom Donati, and Leo Stefanacci for piloting the electronic portfolio process outlined in this book
- Barb Thompson for her efforts in building partnerships between library media specialists and teachers
- The entire Seneca Valley Middle School Team for their support and encouragement
- Most of all, my wife, Amy, and my son, Luke, for allowing me the valuable time needed to invest in this process

Jay D'Ambrosio, M.A.

About the Author

Jay D'Ambrosio teaches Ancient Civilizations at the Seneca Valley Middle School, near Pittsburgh, Pennsylvania. He is the founder and owner of Atlantis Web Solutions, a Web development company specializing in Web and wireless site design, as well as Web management services. Two Web sites designed by D'Ambrosio have been recognized as "Best Bets in Education" by USA Today. He created, taught, and facilitated the E-Teaching: From A to Z workshop as a part of the Pennsylvania Middle School Association. D'Ambrosio has traveled throughout Europe, Mexico, and the South Pacific, and holds a master's degree in history. He currently resides outside of Pittsburgh with his wife, Amy, and their son, Luke.

Foreword

Educators in growing numbers are using portfolios in the form of files, folders, or notebooks in the classroom as authentic assessments. However, the electronic portfolio is now a viable option brought forward by the increased availability of technology in the classroom, providing yet another method for evaluating what students can do. Electronic portfolios go beyond just paper and pencil work — they include varied media such as text, graphics, video, and sound. After all, products on paper constitute only a small portion of what the student produces during the course of a typical school year.

Portfolios bring together curriculum, instruction, and assessment. Through the use of portfolios, teachers and students can jointly develop a shared understanding of standards for quality work, and develop a common language for evaluating students' accomplishments and learning. The use of portfolios helps facilitate classrooms that are student-centered rather than teacher-centered, as students accept more responsibility and become agents in their own education. Teachers and students may construct portfolios in literacy and writing, science, math, the arts, or any other subject area in the curriculum. Portfolios may also be more inclusive, containing samples of work across curricular areas.

Using technology to enhance and simplify portfolio systems is an idea that has been receiving increased attention among educators at all levels. With regard to portfolios, many educators and school districts are in the early planning stages and are finding it advantageous to follow the adage "Think Big — Start Small." Within individual classrooms, the use of electronic portfolios is increasing as teachers explore commercial software designed exclusively for portfolio development, and in times of decreasing budgets, they are using software that is commonly found in most classrooms, such as Microsoft PowerPoint. School districts considering the use of an electronic portfolio, especially one that would involve use of wide area computer networks, are generally in the beginning stages of development with exciting results being generated as students create portfolios that are accessed from year to year, grade level to grade level.

From 1993–1996, six schools were studied that embraced the ideas that "non-techie" people are capable of creating portfolios, portfolios are part of the process of change, and portfolios can be used in multiple contexts (Niguidaula, 26–29). From this study, five key factors were identified in making electronic portfolios work: vision, assessment, technology, logistics, and culture. Key questions must be asked from the perspective of these factors as teachers and districts begin implementing electronic portfolios. The central question under vision is "What should students know and be able to do?" Vision thus becomes the main menu of the portfolio. Four questions apply to assessment: "How can students demonstrate the school vision? Why do we collect student work? What audiences are most important to us? How do we know what's good?" Questions about technology underlie these factors: "What hardware, software, and networking will we need? Who are the primary users of the equipment? Who will support the system?" With regard to logistics, questions asked were: "Where will the information be digitized? Who will do it? Who will select the work? Who will reflect on the work?" The fifth feature, culture, is the most crucial: "Is the school used to discussing student work? Is the school open to sharing standards? With whom?" The researchers concluded that "school culture is perhaps the most critical component in making digital portfolios a tool for reform rather than a technological version of a set of file folders."

The ability to use technology for the development and management of portfolios is now a reality. The electronic portfolio is a tool all students can use to be successful in an information and communication based society, and educators must be committed to exploring its potential.

Louis A. Nagy, Ed.D.
Duquesne University

Introduction

Why Incorporate Web Design and Web Portfolios into the Learning Process?

All life is an experiment. — Ralph Waldo Emerson

A rthur C. Clarke, in *Profiles of the Future*, proposed that any sufficiently advanced technology is indistinguishable from magic (2). Many would tend to identify this statement with a lost tribe in the rain forest that has just witnessed the approach of an airplane or the chatter of a shortwave radio for the first time. Yet, as educators, if we take an honest look at ourselves, we have to admit that some of the instructional technology available for our library media centers and classrooms seems so utterly remote and complex that it almost appears miraculous under the command of a specialist. So why should we bother trying to incorporate such technology into our daily lesson planning? Because our instructional methods must constantly adapt and advance in order to accommodate the needs and modalities of today's students. Web design and student-created Web portfolios are two examples of instructional technology that can significantly reinforce and enhance learning. They are also part of a larger educational movement to incorporate instructional technology into the learning environment, a movement known as "E-Teaching."

The purpose of this book is to demonstrate how library media specialists and teachers can form partnerships to develop educational Web sites and integrate student-centered Web portfolios into the learning process. This book will advocate the use of Microsoft PowerPoint as an important tool for the creation of both types of Web presentations. Further, this book presents a clear and sequential set of directions for the creation of Web sites and Web portfolios.

1. **The Web portfolio process is conducive to student learning in the classroom.**
   A Web portfolio is a purposeful collection of student work in an electronic format, such as a Microsoft PowerPoint® presentation. This electronic portfolio is then placed on a Web server so that it is viewable online. Further information concerning the purpose and development of Web portfolios will be addressed in Chapter 11. The creation of a Web portfolio is a project that significantly improves a student's motivation to learn. Studies have

determined that students are extremely motivated by activities that are inter-active, fun, and personally meaningful (McCombs, 1991, 117–127; 1993, 287–313; 1994, 49–69). Allowing students the opportunity to create their own Web portfolios synthesizes interactivity, fun, and meaning into one ongoing learning strategy.

Web portfolios can also be used as an effective means of alternative assessment, a breath of fresh air for educators who have grown weary of paper and pencil evaluation. Eva L. Baker, of the National Center for Research on Evaluation, Standards, and Student Testing, further supports the assertion that instructional technology, such as Web portfolios, should be interwoven into the curriculum. She emphatically responds to the following questions in an article posted on the U.S. Department of Education Web site: "Does educational technology work? Does its application in classrooms help children learn? Can teachers improve their own understanding and practice through technology? Yes! Yes!! And yes!!!" ("Technology: How Do We Know It Works?," par. 1).

2. **An educational Web site meets the needs of visual learners.**
Educators are noticing that many of the young people we work with are increasingly being identified as visual learners. Ramlee Mustapha relates in his online article, *Diverse Learners in Vocational and Technical Education: Strategies for Success*, that close to eight out of every ten students today are primarily visual learners (6). Some attribute the rise in this particular modality to the spread of MTV and graphic intensive video game systems. Whatever the reason, we as educators find ourselves in the position of competing for our students' attention visually. When we learn to harness the power of Web design, this arduous challenge becomes easier to meet.

An educational Web site that incorporates pictures, graphics, sound, or video is much more likely to get and hold students' attention than the traditional textbook and worksheet method. Dr. Barbara Means, in an online Stanford International Research Institute news release, declares, "The Web can make it possible for students to learn in the context of working on real-world problems, can help connect students to experts and a community of learners, and can provide tools and support for rigorous thinking" ("Barbara Means, Co-Director Of SRI International's Center For Technology In Learning, Participates In Congressional Web-Based Education Commission Hearing" par. 4). An educator who is determined to create an environment where true learning can take place must take advantage of the opportunities offered by Web design and the Web portfolio process. A library media specialist can greatly influence teachers' decisions about how they make use of this powerful educational tool, and serve as a mentor and teaching partner to integrate the Web into teaching and learning.

3. **As educators, we need to keep pace with technological and cultural changes to maintain relevance for our students.**
Over the past decade, our society has undergone a "change," a revolution so extreme and irreversible that communication and commerce as we know it

today would seem next to impossible without it. This "change" is commonly referred to as the Internet. As educators, we must come to grips with the fact that a large proportion of our students are among the half billion Internet users worldwide!

On January 8, 2002, President Bush signed the No Child Left Behind (NCLB) Act. This law officially reauthorizes the 1965 Elementary and Secondary Education (ESEA) Act. One of the programs within the ESEA, known as Enhancing Education Through Technology (Ed Tech), has the primary goal of improving student academic performance through the use of technology in school. According to the U.S. Department of Education's document, *Guidance on the Enhancing Education Through Technology (Ed Tech) Program*, the goal of this program is "to improve student academic achievement through the use of technology in elementary and secondary schools. This law is designed to promote technology literacy among all students by the end of eighth grade — regardless of race, ethnicity, income, geographical location, or disability. This law also encourages the effective integration of technology resources and systems with professional development and curriculum development to promote research-based instructional methods that can be widely replicated" (2). Kristin Loschert, in an article published in *NEA Today* entitled *Are You Ready*, states that Ed Tech focuses on three goals:

- improving student academic achievement through the use of technology,
- assisting students in becoming technologically literate by the time they finish eighth grade, and
- ensuring that teachers can integrate technology into the curriculum (9).

Thus, library media specialists and teachers must familiarize themselves with various electronic media so that they are able to deliver instruction in a way that is both significant and relevant to those they intend to educate. Most experts today foresee the application of the Internet in our daily lives in ways that we can scarcely imagine. To avoid becoming obsolete, educators must learn to use electronic resources as tools to enhance instruction.

Content and Features of This Book

As was mentioned, technology and its application in the classroom can appear overwhelming upon first glance, so Part I of this book will focus on a simple method of Web design for librarians and teachers using Microsoft PowerPoint. This program provides a vehicle for librarians and teachers to create educational Web sites and participate in the ever-growing world of cyberspace. Moreover, it affords students the opportunity to utilize higher-order thinking skills through the creation of Web portfolios in a way that studies have shown to be highly motivational. Thus, the book will include a clear and applicable method for library media specialists and teachers to create their own Web sites, customized to meet the needs of their specific curriculum using this software. One cautionary note: The steps outlined in this book may need to be slightly modified depending upon which version of Microsoft PowerPoint is being utilized.

The benefits of creating student Web portfolios will be discussed in Part II, as well as methods for the development of such electronic portfolios. The reader will be able to use this book as a guide to developing educational Web sites and student Web portfolios. The book will include Mini Glossaries at the end of most chapters that will assist the reader in defining important keywords used throughout those chapters. Furthermore, sections known as Library Media Connections will be interspersed throughout the book, offering insight on ways in which library media specialists and teachers can collaborate to develop educational Web sites and a student Web portfolio system.

A variety of fictional educator-created Web sites are discussed in Chapter 1 to examine how each one is used in the learning process. Chapter 2 focuses on Microsoft PowerPoint and the advantages of using this particular software in this cutting-edge endeavor. Hardware and software issues are important to consider before beginning this effort, so these issues are addressed in Chapter 3. Instructions for using Microsoft PowerPoint are provided in Chapters 4–9, including the addition of display slides; changing background colors and patterns; the incorporation of text, hyperlinks, images, image effects, and animation; and publishing the presentation to the Web. These same instructions can then be passed along to the students when they begin the Web portfolio process. Chapter 10 presents several ideas for promoting a Web site.

Part II deals exclusively with issues surrounding the implementation of Web portfolios into the learning process. Chapter 11 addresses the purpose of portfolios in general, and then cites the advantages of electronic portfolios over more traditional portfolio systems. Ideas concerning the content of Web portfolios are discussed in Chapter 12. Finally, Chapters 13 and 14 focus on the practicalities of using the computer lab or library media center and its resources, as well as the presentation and assessment of Web portfolios.

Mini Glossary

Internet A worldwide network connecting millions of computers for communications purposes.

Multimedia Refers to audio, video, animation, graphics, or a combination of these.

Portfolio A collection of a student's work and learning experiences for the purposes of reflection and assessment.

Web Page or Web Site A document or group of electronic documents that can be accessed through the Internet.

World Wide Web or WWW or Web An interface for the Internet, made up of computers that provide access to documents that further provide access to other documents, multimedia files, and Web pages.

PART I

Teacher-Created Web Sites

Give a man a fish and he will eat for a day.
Teach a man to fish and he will eat for the rest of his life. —Chinese Proverb

Chapter 1

Examples of Effective Teacher-Created Web Sites

The whole art of teaching is only the art of awakening the natural curiosity of young minds for the purpose of satisfying it afterwards. — Anatole France

To design an effective educational Web site, the Web site's creator must establish a clear purpose for the Web site's existence. To establish the purpose of a Web site, consider the following questions:

- What information should the Web site contain?
- How will this information further student learning in the educational environment?
- What should the students be able to "do" with the Web site?

To find the answers to these questions, it is often helpful to examine Web sites created by other teachers or library media specialists and the part these Web sites play in enriching instruction. By evaluating several fictitious teacher-created sites, you will be able to further establish the manner in which you can use a Web site within the framework of a particular educational setting.

Informational Sites

The most basic kind of teacher-created Web site is known as an informational site. An informational site can provide standard information about a teacher, as well as the course or courses that the teacher instructs. This type of Web site often includes the following components:

- Home page
- Teacher's background and contact information page
- Syllabus or course outline page
- Classroom rules page
- Materials needed throughout the year page
- Message to the parent's page
- Favorite links to other Web sites page

The following example will allow you to further investigate the informational Web site in a more visual manner, using a sample site known as "Mr. Nguyen's French Class Web Site."

Home Page

The home page is the first page in a Web site. The purpose of the home page is to 1) entice visitors to further explore the other pages within the Web site, and 2) to provide information about what is included on the site. An effective home page should include the title of the site, an image or images related to the site, and hyperlinks to other pages within the Web site. In this example, Mr. Nguyen has incorporated an image of the Eiffel Tower to emphasize the focus of this Web site.

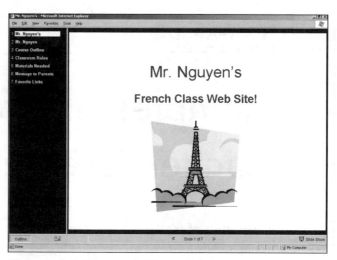

Figure 1.1: Nguyen's Home Page

Teacher's Background and Contact Information

This section of the informational Web site often communicates a brief background about the instructor. This does not necessarily need to be a resume, just the highlights and the qualities about the teacher that are important to the course being taught. Here, Mr. Nguyen includes length of service, travel experience, educational background, hobbies, and interests. This component should usually offer the visitor to the site an avenue of communication with the site's author, such as an e-mail address, phone number, mailing address, or all of these.

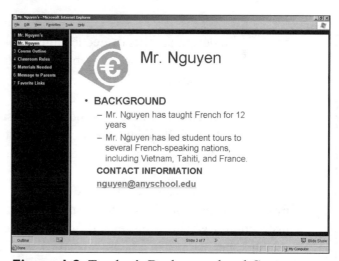

Figure 1.2: Teacher's Background and Contact Information

Syllabus or Course Outline

This part of the informational Web site usually showcases the highlights of the course through a course outline or a syllabus. Mr. Nguyen uses this as an efficient way to communicate the goals of the course to both parents and students.

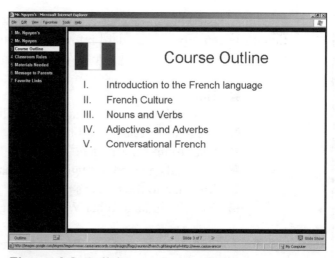

Figure 1.3: Syllabus or Course Outline

Classroom Rules

An important part of an informational Web site that many teachers find useful is a classroom rules page. Adding a classroom rules section allows Mr. Nguyen to direct students and parents to the Web to understand his expectations; this is more efficient than developing printed handouts that may or may not reach the parents.

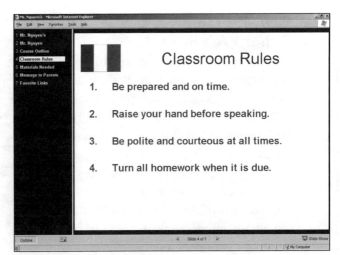

Figure 1.4: Classroom Rules

Materials Needed

Many teachers choose to include a page that lists the materials needed for their course. This page is beneficial for making sure that students are well prepared for the class. In addition, the page can be made accessible to parents before the start of the school year.

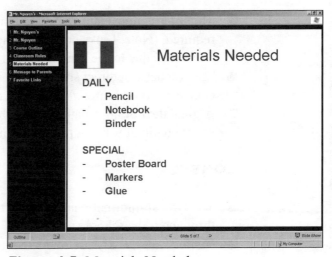

Figure 1.5: Materials Needed

Message to the Parents

Educators who have taken the time to develop an informational Web site sometimes incorporate a message to the parents of their students. This can help to further explain the purposes of the course while at the same time adding a more personal dimension. Mr. Nguyen has delivered his message to the parents in the form of a letter.

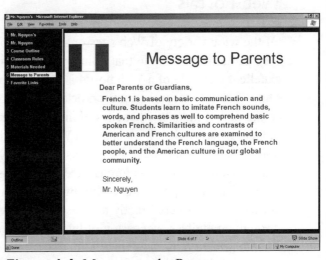

Figure 1.6: Message to the Parents

Favorite Links to Other Web Sites

Visitors to a Web site often return to the site largely due to the links that are displayed there. Visitors who find those links useful tend to make that site a regular browsing point. Mr. Nguyen has provided links to some practical Web sites, including dictionaries and translators.

Now that we have explored the components of the informational site, we will examine the pros and cons of creating a site such as this.

Figure 1.7: Favorite Links to Other Web Sites

PROS

- The informational site is easy to maintain. Little work outside of initial setup is required. (Note: Links posted on any Web site need to be regularly maintained and monitored due to the fluid nature of online content.)
- The teacher can direct students and parents to the Web site when questions about the course are raised throughout the year.
- A great deal of information about the course can be conveyed to a large number of people without wasting paper or print resources.

CONS

- The typical informational Web site tends to be static, meaning that it rarely changes throughout the school year.
- Visitors can quickly tire of a site that does not offer anything new.
- Students without computers or Internet access at home will be unable to access an informational site outside of the library media center or classroom.

Web Portals

Of the wide variety of Web sites online, few do more to draw visitors than Web portals. The Web portal is a Web site that points visitors to other Web sites via an organized directory. An excellent example of a Web portal is Kathy Schrock's (Guide for Educators) Web site <http://school.discovery.com/schrockguide/>. It is essentially a Web site that is almost entirely comprised of links to other sites of interest for educators from around the Internet. The University of California, Berkeley, maintains a Web portal featuring links to national and international libraries and library sites <http://sunsite.berkeley.edu/LibWeb/>. Many teachers and librarians have found that a site of this nature is exceptionally useful for student research assignments.

The Web portal generally divides the links listed on the site into several categories. This allows visitors to go directly to the section in which they are most interested, without scrolling through an endless succession of hyperlinks. Following is a fictional Web portal, known as *Ms. Washington's Literature Portal*.

Ms. Washington's Web portal begins, as any effective Web site should, with an eye-catching home page. The link categories are neatly arrayed on the left, and a title, created in a fancy font, decorates the top of the page. The picture on the home page brings to mind a scene from one of the books that her class is reading. Each link on the left takes the visitor to further links to other sites related to that particular topic:

Within the link category entitled *The Diary of Anne Frank*, Ms. Washington has selected various Web sites that relate to issues raised as her class reads the book. Located to the right of each link is a brief description of the site to which the visitor will be connected. Not every Web portal contains descriptions next to links. However, this is a recommended time-saving feature that enables visitors to avoid clicking through links to find the one they want. By pre-selecting links, the quality of the information available for student use increases significantly.

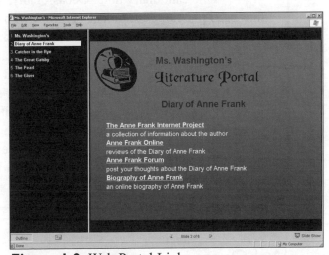

Figure 1.8: Web Portal Home Page

Figure 1.9: Web Portal Links

PROS

- The Web portal site places a great deal of strong information and online resources at a student's fingertips.
- The Web portal keeps visitors coming back to the site to visit their favorite links about various subjects.
- This type of site is a valuable research tool for class projects and reports.

CONS

- The Web portal does not provide much original content; rather, it is a gateway to other resources that are available online.
- The initial setup of a Web portal requires a bit of online investigation, finding Web sites that are age appropriate and relevant to each topic.
- Some Web sites dealing with specific subject matter appear to have been created by a content area specialist, when in reality information can be false or misleading. For example, someone who has a passing interest in the discovery of King Tutankhamen's tomb may design a Web site that appears to speak with authority on the topic. Seek out the designer's credentials and experience. You should attempt to

contact the individual who has created the site in question via e-mail to obtain more information regarding the nature of the site.

■ The content of the Web sites that are linked to is often out of the control of the educator. This means that if the substance of a particular Web site that you have linked to changes, it may render that site inappropriate for students. Links also need to be regularly monitored to ascertain whether they have become "dead" or inaccurate due to the continually changing nature of the World Wide Web. Constant vigilance is required!

Library Media Connection

A Web portal is an ideal site for a library media specialist to develop. Links can be categorized according to subject area, and constantly updated and expanded. This would be an invaluable resource for teachers, students, administrators, and librarians!

One cautionary note: Occasionally, adult Web sites will purchase domain names that used to belong to student-oriented Web sites. When possible, try to link to Web sites that are well known and trusted. Domain names that end in .edu often contain reliable information because this domain indicates an educational institution. However, some colleges and universities allow students and other nonfaculty members to post information on their Web server, which may render site content questionable. Librarians and teachers should collaborate to select Web sites that may be appropriate for a Web portal. Carefully check each Web site before linking to it!

As we discuss the next few Web site styles, we will peer into several hypothetical classrooms to see the ways in which students and teachers use various Web sites to enrich the learning experience.

WebQuest

Nothing tends to motivate learners more than a hint of adventure. A WebQuest is a Web site that asks questions and allows the students to play the detectives, trying to search out answers for themselves. At the San Diego State University WebQuest Web site, Bernie Dodge, professor of educational technology, defines a WebQuest as "an inquiry-oriented activity in which most or all of the information used by learners is drawn from the Web" ("What's A WebQuest?," par. 2). A WebQuest typically requires a student to conduct research online using carefully pre-selected links. The research culminates with a final project or assignment that demonstrates that the student has achieved the stated learning objectives. Almost every WebQuest contains five important features:

1. Introduction
2. Task
3. Process
4. Conclusion
5. Evaluation

Introduction
The introduction presents the purpose of the WebQuest. It can also provide the background information that the students will need to know before they begin. The hypothetical WebQuest

that we will be discussing shortly is *Mr. Vincente's Current Events WebQuest*. The introduction for this WebQuest reads: "Many important issues affect our world today. From politics to the conflict in the Middle East, we must investigate these issues that serve to shape and define modern society. By participating in this current events WebQuest, you will hopefully gain a better understanding of the world around you."

Task

The task explains in general terms what the students will be required to accomplish. For example, if the WebQuest focuses on current events, the task might read: "The students will gain a greater appreciation for important issues facing our world today." The task usually acts as a general learning objective or goal.

Process

Typically the process is divided into several clearly defined missions or sets of directions that guide the student toward the objective or goal. We will take a closer look at the process by examining *Mr. Vincente's Current Events WebQuest*. This fictional WebQuest contains six mission or direction sets. The direction sets/missions for Mr. Vincente's WebQuest are as follows:

Mr. Vincente wanted to create a home page for his WebQuest that was similar to his chalkboard in the classroom. For his title, he chose a font that appears to be written in chalk. His current events topics are arranged along the side, allowing his students to choose which WebQuest they would like to attempt. Maria and Jeremy chose the WebQuest entitled "Politics." Following is what they experienced:

After Maria read the first mission, "Using the White House Web site, find out who is the current Chief of Staff," she clicked on the link entitled "White House." She was taken to the official Web site of the White House, where she did not immediately see the answer to the question. This placed Maria in a position where she had to learn how to navigate the White House Web site. Following some trial and error, she learned how to successfully navigate the site, and found the information.

Jeremy read the second mission and quickly arrived at the Reuters Politics Web site. He found, read, and wrote a brief summary of the first article, which was about the upcoming November elections. Once the summary

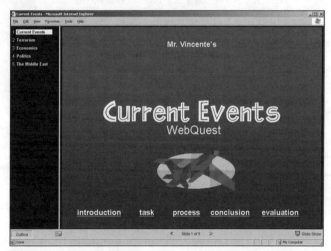

Figure 1.10: WebQuest Home Page

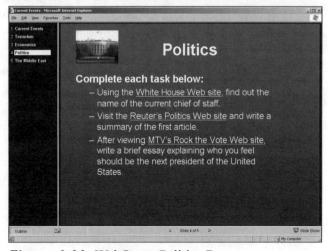

Figure 1.11: WebQuest Politics Page

had been completed, he and Maria turned their attention to the third mission to complete the WebQuest.

Once mission number three had been reviewed, the partners visited the Web site of MTV's "Rock the Vote." They read articles about the road to the White House, watched political ad videos, and listened to campaign sound bites. Maria found herself siding with the Republican candidate, but she also appreciated what the Reform Party candidate had to say. Jeremy was wholeheartedly behind the Democratic candidate. However, the Green Party candidate really made him think. In the end, Maria and Jeremy had a lively debate about which candidate should occupy the nation's highest office for the next four years. They decided to write two journal entry essays, each trying to understand the other's point of view.

Once the Politics WebQuest had been successfully completed, Maria and Jeremy both decided to try the Middle East WebQuest. Maria read the first mission aloud as Jeremy listened intently. They then clicked on the hyperlink leading to the Central Intelligence Agency's World Fact Book Web site. There they learned that the major issue dividing many Arab nations and the nation of Israel is religion. Jeremy was already aware of how important religious differences are in that part of the world, but for Maria, this was somewhat of an eye opener.

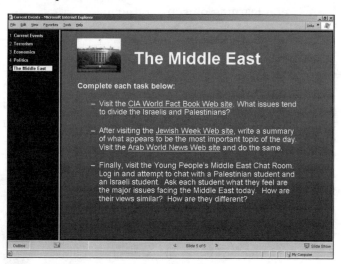

Figure 1.12: WebQuest Middle East Page

The next mission explained that the partners were to visit both an Arab and a Jewish online news outlet to observe which stories made headlines. As the two read the major stories of the day, two different perspectives emerged within the writings. The mission further required that the partners discuss why the two news services contained strikingly different points of view. The information Jeremy and Maria learned in the first mission helped to explain the opposing points of view.

Reading the final Middle East mission, the two Web adventurers looked at each other with some hesitation. Mr. Vincente, who peered quietly over their shoulders, knew that this last mission would nudge his students out of their comfort zone. They were told to visit the Young People's Middle East Message Board. Once there, Jeremy and Maria knew that they had to find a message posted by a young person from both Israel and an Arab nation. After some time, they were able to find a statement from an Israeli student named Avi. They also located a message from a Palestinian student who was living in Jordan. Jeremy and Maria read through the differing points of view for quite a while, considering the problems faced by those living in this part of the world. Mr. Vincente smiled as he watched his students expand their horizons without ever leaving the comfort of their seats.

In this example, it becomes apparent how a WebQuest can spark students' curiosity about the world around them. The World Wide Web is brimming with information, much that is useful, as well as much that is not. A WebQuest focuses a student's efforts, harnessing useful Internet resources, while avoiding those that are less valuable. Educational standards can also be a focus of a WebQuest, using the information contained within certain Web sites as a means to an end. Once educators begin to understand what makes their students tick on a personal level, they can tailor the WebQuest missions to suit the students' individual interests, as well as meet curricular objectives.

Conclusion

The purpose of the conclusion of a WebQuest is to briefly summarize what the student should have learned by completing the WebQuest. Mr. Vincente's conclusion is as follows: "You have learned that a number of important issues influence our modern world. You have investigated topics such as politics, terrorism, and the Middle East. Hopefully, through your participation in this current events WebQuest, you have gained a greater appreciation for the often complex issues that change and affect the world today." Being an actual lesson, a WebQuest requires some form of closure to reinforce stated objectives. The conclusion serves as a lesson closure for a WebQuest project.

Evaluation

The evaluation method can vary from teacher to teacher. It is important that the form of evaluation be clearly communicated to students prior to beginning the WebQuest so that they will understand what is required. Some teachers will choose to have the students complete a long or short-term project based on information learned throughout the WebQuest. Other teachers, following completion of the WebQuest, may decide to have the students write a journal response, create a skit, compose a song, or draw a picture. Using the information gathered during the WebQuest, teachers might elect to have the students complete any of the following assignments:

- Write and deliver an informative or persuasive speech.
- Compose a song, rap, or poem.
- Paint or draw a picture or poster.
- Create a skit.
- Develop a bulletin board.
- Write an obituary.
- Create a chart, graph, or diagram.
- Construct a time line or map of an area.
- Write a newspaper article or letter to the editor.
- Perform an experiment.
- Conduct a survey.
- Participate in a panel discussion.
- Create a travel brochure.
- Develop a game.
- Create a video documentary.
- Conduct a pro and con debate.

It is also possible to evaluate the success or failure of the WebQuest missions without a culminating project or assignment. This could be accomplished through the use of a simple rubric, such as that shown in Figure 1.12a on page 16.

An important aspect of WebQuests is that they are highly adaptable to a specific curriculum. If a teacher wishes to place a special focus on a certain type of assessment, a WebQuest can be easily modified to fit almost any requirements.

PROS

- WebQuests are highly motivational. Studies show that students are strongly motivated by assignments that are interactive and meaningful to them as individuals (McCombs, 1991, 117–127; 1993, 287–313; 1994, 49–69).
- WebQuests are easy to mold to any curriculum because the teacher formulates the questions or missions to achieve specific learning outcomes.
- Students learn information literacy skills such as navigating and integrating information from Web sites, skills that may be useful later in life.

CONS

- WebQuests require a teacher or a library media specialist to construct questions or missions, and locate online resources that students can use to complete each mission. This can be time-consuming.
- Educators are creating hyperlinks to Web sites that are beyond their control. This requires constant vigilance.

WebQuest Rubric					
	4	**3**	**2**	**1**	**Points**
Introduction	All questions were answered	Most questions were answered	Some questions were answered	Few questions were answered	
Task	All missions were attempted	Most missions were attempted	Some missions were attempted	Few missions were attempted	
Process	All team members worked together	Most team members worked together	Some team members worked together	Few team members worked together	
Grammar & Spelling	There were no grammar and/or spelling errors	There were few grammar and/or spelling errors	There were some grammar and/or spelling errors	There were many grammar and/or spelling errors	
Creativity	All questions were answered creatively	Most questions were answered creatively	Some questions were answered creatively	Few questions were answered creatively	
				TOTAL	

Figure 1.12a: WebQuest Rubric

Being familiar with school policy toward certain Web sites such as chat rooms or online forums, the library media specialist should guide teachers through the process of selecting Web sites that are suitable for inclusion in a WebQuest project. The school librarian is also a curriculum specialist who is capable of drawing connections between various disciplines and identifying proper learning outcomes. A WebQuest is an ideal learning strategy for an interdisciplinary endeavor! As an instructional partner, the library media specialist can work with a teacher to develop WebQuest tasks, as well as a form of assessment that accurately measures the degree to which instructional goals are met.

Virtual Field Trip

These days, many school districts find themselves bound by financial constraints. Organizing a field trip to a museum, science center, or play can be a costly experience for students and teachers. Many variables must be considered, such as scheduling, district policy, bus transportation, lunch arrangements, and the distribution of student medication. However, nothing truly compares to visiting and experiencing a site firsthand, so field trips remain a vital part of the educational experience.

If teachers wish to bring into their classroom the sense of discovery that often accompanies the traditional field trip, there is a solution. A virtual field trip or virtual tour is a dynamic Web site that fosters learning by arousing the curiosity of the learner and simulating the experience of a real field trip. The virtual field trip model centers on a specific location that could not otherwise be visited by the student. For example, a student would never be able to take a field trip to the Sun. A poor rural school district in Kentucky would be unlikely to visit a Mayan archaeological dig in Mexico. A student from inner city Chicago may never have the opportunity to stare in wonder at the Great Wall of China. By creating a virtual field trip, a teacher is able to deliver the next best thing right into the classroom or school.

The following example, known as "Ms. Matambo's Virtual Field Trip to the Great Barrier Reef," will demonstrate how a Web site such as this can be incorporated into a typical science classroom:

Ms. Matambo had traveled to Australia's Great Barrier Reef during the summer before her senior year of college. While teaching the concept of classification to her seventh grade science class, one of her students asked a question that brought that long-ago trip to the forefront of her mind. The student wondered where on our planet someone could go to find a species that has not yet been discovered. Ms. Matambo paused for a moment and recalled the vast diversity of life she witnessed firsthand while scuba diving near the Great Barrier Reef. With that one question, Ms. Matambo's "Virtual Field Trip to the Great Barrier Reef" Web site was conceived.

Cassie, the student who asked the pivotal question, looked at the homework assignment directions with growing interest. Cassie had always lacked motivation when it came to completing homework. Yes, she had heard all the reasons why she should be more focused on her studies, but all she really seemed to look forward to anymore was talking to her friends online through an instant messaging system. Homework definitely came in a distant second. However, as she read the directions for this assignment, things changed—this assignment seemed to be something that she could "get into."

As Cassie sat in front of her computer at home later that afternoon, she began to type the URL that Ms. Matambo had specified into the location bar. Upon seeing the home page, Cassie knew that this was going to be an assignment unlike any other. After taking a virtual field trip to Australia's Great Barrier Reef, she was required to classify the different forms of life highlighted throughout the Web site. It might even be fun!

She began by clicking on the link to the left, entitled "Sharks of Australia Exhibit."

Looking through the online shark exhibit, Cassie realized that she had never really thought about all of the different shark species that exist in the oceans. She also learned that contrary to popular opinion, many sharks are not dangerous to humans.

Cassie then moved on to the next link, which was the "Invertebrate Exhibit." The only invertebrates she had ever thought about were the worms that appeared on the sidewalk after a good drenching rain.

Invertebrates had often repulsed Cassie because she thought them to be nothing more than slimy worm-like creatures. However, the "Invertebrate Exhibit" in the virtual field trip had made her realize that many invertebrates were amazing and beautiful.

When Cassie clicked on the link "Coral Exhibit," she noticed another hyperlink leading her to a video where she could watch the formation of a coral reef over the course of thousands of years through computer animation.

Through watching the video, Cassie began to appreciate how long it takes a coral reef to form and how important a reef is to an underwater ecosystem. She also started to comprehend that many coral reefs are

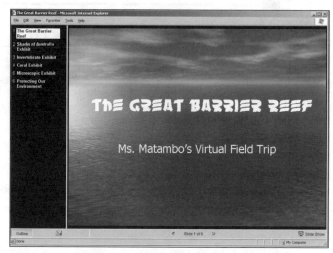

Figure 1.13: Virtual Field Trip Home Page

Figure 1.14: Virtual Field Trip—Sharks of Australia

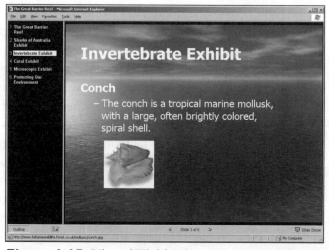

Figure 1.15: Virtual Field Trip—Invertebrate Exhibit

threatened by human development, not to mention naturally occurring phenomena such as El Niño, which can decrease the oxygen content in the water, slowly killing the reef.

Cassie later browsed through two other online exhibits. One focused on microscopic organisms and their relationship to the food chain of the Great Barrier Reef, while the other emphasized the importance of protecting the environment, especially the coral reefs of the world. Reflecting on the afternoon virtual field trip to the Great Barrier Reef, Cassie wrote in her science journal that she felt in some small way that her horizons had been broadened, and that she now had a greater sense of wonder toward the world around her.

Figure 1.16: Virtual Field Trip—Coral Exhibit

PROS

- Virtual field trips are a method by which teachers can take students to see a place or even a time period which cannot be experienced or is unlikely to be experienced.
- Unlike real field trips, virtual field trips can be designed with students in mind.
- The educator controls what the students experience.
- Virtual field trips allow the students to experience a sense of being able to "wander" and learn at the same time.

CONS

- Virtual field trips require online research to set them up correctly. The teacher or library media specialist must first find Web sites and online activities that directly relate to the virtual field trip. This can be time-consuming.
- Virtual field trips should ideally be visually engaging. This means that whenever possible, images should be incorporated into the Web site to give the student the feeling of being present at the location. This requires that the teacher search for images online, which can also be time-consuming.

Library Media Connection

Library media specialists can guide teachers through the process of developing a virtual field trip by creating a directory or database of photographs. Many distributors offer royalty-free stock photography on CD-ROM for such purposes. If library collections include such resources, this can greatly reduce online time requirements. As interdisciplinary specialists, librarians can readily identify the needs of different departments in this area, and collect digitized photographs or purchase commercial databases to meet these needs.

Photo Gallery

Someone once said that there are three great things about teaching—June, July, and August. While anyone who sincerely loves the teaching profession would say that there are many reasons to consider a career in education, most would agree that summer offers much needed time for rest and reflection. Many teachers use their summer leave as an opportunity to do just that . . . leave. Travel is a popular pastime among educators during the summer months. An excursion to some exotic port-of-call is usually documented photographically.

Traditionally, teachers have attempted to show slides of their voyage to foreign countries or their exploration of historical sites. Now just for a moment, put yourself back into the shoes of an elementary, middle, or high school student. Imagine your teacher setting up the slide projector as you ease into your seat before the late bell rings. Are you excited at the prospect of watching a slide show while your teacher narrates? Most likely you are not. Why? Well, one important reason is that you are not an active participant in this learning experience; you are in a passive role. Studies have shown that allowing students to make choices within a project leads to active learning (Johnston and Allington, 984–1012).

The photo gallery site offers an attractive alternative to this problem. The name itself is fairly self-explanatory. This is a Web site that is intended to display photographs taken by a teacher or student. A nice feature about a photo gallery Web site is that the teacher or students can view the photographs they would like to see, when they want to see them. This allows special needs students, who may not cognitively process information at the same rate as other students, the ability to browse the images at a slower, more comfortable pace. Perhaps some students merely enjoy viewing a photograph for an extended period of time to "immerse" themselves in the picture. In the following section, we will consider another hypothetical Web site entitled "Mr. Singh's Photo Gallery:"

For years, Mr. Singh had spent his summers traveling to different cities across the United States. He had grown up in Toronto, Canada, and had always enjoyed the fast paced excitement of urban living. He moved to the United States to accept a teaching position in an elementary school in Hope, Arkansas. When he arrived, Mr. Singh spent a great deal of time getting to know the students he was teaching. He realized that many of his students had never visited a big city, nor did they possess any concept of what one was like.

The next day, Mr. Singh brought his photo album into class. With pride, Mr. Singh opened the cover and began pointing out pictures of massive highway systems, bridges, sky-scrapers, and museums. However, he found that several of his students complained that they could not see the pictures, and wanted to move closer. They ended up crowding out others who also wanted to see the photographs. Some students appeared disinterested, while others were simply frustrated because they felt left out of the viewing.

That evening, Mr. Singh thought about his experience with the photo album in his class-room. He knew that there had to be a better way to present his photographs, so as to create a learning experience for his students. While searching the Internet for possible solutions, he came across an idea that seemed to be the perfect solution: a photo gallery Web site. The first step was to digitize (convert into an electronic format) his photographs, or transform his pictures into something that a computer can understand. To accomplish that goal, the library media specialist at his elementary school suggested that he use the library's scanner to input the images into a computer. He guided Mr. Singh through this endeavor, but it did take some time, since he had taken so many photographs. However, in the end it was well worth the effort.

Once the photographs had been digitized, Mr. Singh was able to construct his photo gallery Web site. When he escorted his students to the school's computer lab, they were surprised at what they found.

Mr. Singh encouraged each student to choose a city and browse through the images. Danny, a nine-year-old Steelers fan, decided to stay true to his football team, so he chose Pittsburgh.

Danny thought the photographs he saw were cool. He wanted to visit Pittsburgh in person someday, but for now the photographs were enough. His classmate, Shannon, decided that she would like to look at the Chicago photo set. A member of an Irish-American family, her grandfather had been a part of the Chicago police department. She wanted to view what she thought of as pictures of her family's heritage.

Mr. Singh found that his students were much more engaged in this lesson than in the previous one that involved the use of his photo album. Now, Mr. Singh owns a digital camera and saves his photographs to his computer hard drive. This has made the process much easier and highly rewarding.

PROS

- A photo gallery Web site enables students to browse photographs at their own pace.
- Photo gallery Web sites do not require the teacher to present the images through a traditional slide show.
- Students can choose which images they wish to browse, when they wish to do so. Research has demonstrated that allowing a student to make choices within an

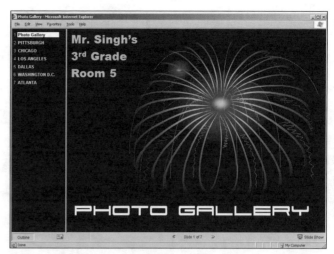

Figure 1.17: Photo Gallery Home Page

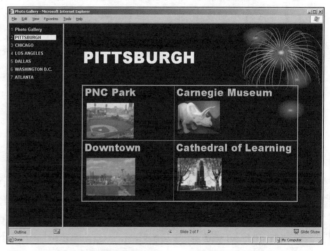

Figure 1.18: Photo Gallery—Pittsburgh

Figure 1.19: Photo Gallery—Chicago

assignment leads to more effective learning (Johnston and Allington, 1991, 984–1012).

CONS

- If a teacher has many photographs, creating a photo gallery Web site can be a daunting task.
- If the photographs are in print form, rather than digital, they will need to be scanned, which can become a tedious undertaking, especially if there are many photographs.

Library Media Connection

The library media center should offer a wide range of options for the creation of digital photographs. If teachers have print photographs that need to be converted into a digital format, they will need to be scanned. If teachers have yet to take the photographs, they can use a digital camera. Many teachers are hesitant to use such technology due to lack of experience. Because librarians specialize in the application of instructional technology, they can provide professional development options for educators interested in learning more about taking digital photographs or digitizing print photographs.

Topical Site

Every subject, whether it be reading, health, mathematics, English, social studies, science, or physical education, can be arranged topically. The standard curriculum for each subject carries with it expectations that throughout the length of the course, certain topics or themes will be taught. Many state legislatures are mandating that specific standards be met in a variety of subject areas. In today's schools, teachers often find that instructional time is being decreased, while at the same time, they are being asked to do more and more. This can create quite a dilemma for new educators and veterans alike. How does one meet the requirements of the curriculum while managing the extra duties and obligations necessitated by district policy, state mandate, and federal acts?

The topical Web site offers a solution for educators who would like to teach a specific curricular point in more detail, but lack the time in the classroom. This particular Web site highlights a specific topic covered within a larger course. For example, if the subject being taught is science, then the topical Web site might focus on plate tectonics. If the subject is health, then the topical Web site could shine a spotlight on hygiene. A social studies teacher, who teaches a course entitled Early American History, might create a topical Web site about the settlement of Jamestown. A kindergarten teacher may decide to design a topical Web site concerning holidays or seasons. Topical Web sites are as vast and varied as the curriculum they stem from and the teachers or library media specialists who design them. Following is a topical Web site created by a fictitious physical education teacher known as Miss Adams. The name of the Web site is "Miss Adams' Volleyball Web Site."

Miss Adams played volleyball for the University of Michigan and was a starter for three years. Those days of intense competition were over, but the love for the game lived on. She had always enjoyed the volleyball unit that she taught to her students each year. However, the demands of the curriculum and the interruptions of the school year always seemed to hinder her ability to really delve into the strategy of the game. Far too often it seemed that as soon as the students began to comprehend the rules, covering required district standards necessitated moving on to another sporting event.

Figure 1.20: Topical Web Site Home Page

This lack of time and subsequent lack of knowledge gained denied many students an opportunity to decide whether they might like to try out for the school's volleyball team. As the school's junior varsity volleyball coach, Miss Adams was determined to rectify this situation. She began by creating a Web site devoted to a better understanding of the sport of volleyball. To add a personal touch, she decorated the site in the colors of her alma mater. With the help of her library media specialist, she found clip art of a ball going over the net from a CD-ROM and added it to the home page. She then divided the Web site into several Web pages dedicated to different aspects of the game. Along the left-hand frame, she displayed the links to each page: bumping, setting, spiking, serving, formations, the rules, and links.

Once the site was complete, Miss Adams came up with a plan for letting her students know that it was available. The last day of the volleyball unit had finally arrived. Many of her students found that they enjoyed the game and wanted to learn more. Miss Adams had prepared flyers to let students know about the new Web site.

Two of Miss Adams' students, Da'Lynn and Stasi, were intrigued by the flier. Both girls had enjoyed playing volleyball during their physical education class, but they had never

Do you want to learn more about volleyball?

Are you thinking about joining the school's volleyball team?

If so, visit the Web site below:

www._____.com

Figure 1.21: Web Site Flier

considered exploring the sport further. At home that evening, Da'Lynn turned on her computer and typed the Web address into the location bar. When Miss Adams' Volleyball Web Site appeared, she began by clicking on the first link, "Bumping." She then moved on to the other links to learn tips and tricks for getting the most out of your serve, set, or spike. Finally she clicked on the link labeled "Links." Here she found a list of other Web sites that offered additional information about volleyball, as well as links to various community volleyball leagues.

Da'Lynn was still hesitant to try out for the school's volleyball team, but she gave some serious thought to the community league teams available. She talked to her friend Stasi on the phone that night about joining a volleyball league. Stasi had visited Miss Adams' Web site as well. The next day, the girls walked to the community recreation center and signed up for a beginner's volleyball league.

PROS

- A topical Web site allows a teacher to provide access to additional information both inside and outside the classroom.
- Topical Web sites often enable an educator to cover curricular material in greater depth than would otherwise be possible in the classroom.
- Topical Web sites can be utilized as a learning resource for multiple teachers.

CONS

- Topical Web sites are limited to specific topics and are not often used after a unit has been completed.

Teachers occasionally utilize stories to emphasize certain points with their students. Oftentimes, these stories can communicate concepts and ideas in a more permanent and meaningful manner. Hopefully, the above story-form examples have provided ideas about the ways in which a teacher-created Web site can be used to supplement a particular curriculum.

Mini Glossary

E-Mail	A message sent to a person or group electronically through the Internet.
Home Page	The first Web page of a Web site that a visitor will see—usually the most important page.
URL	Uniform Resource Locator. A technical term for a Web address or domain name.
Web Browser or Browser	A type of software, such as Internet Explorer or Netscape Navigator, that locates and displays a Web page.

Chapter 2

Why Use Microsoft PowerPoint® to Create Teacher Web Sites?

Go confidently in the direction of your dreams.
Live the life you have imagined.—Henry David Thoreau

You may be wondering why you are being encouraged to use Microsoft PowerPoint as a Web design tool. If you happen to have some experience designing Web sites, you have probably noticed that Microsoft PowerPoint does not usually appear on anybody's list of suggested Web editing software. If one is preparing to develop a Web site, software such as Microsoft FrontPage®, Macromedia Dreamweaver®, Claris Home Page®, and Netscape Composer® seem to be the logical choices of most Web designers. However, it will soon become apparent that Microsoft PowerPoint is an extremely effective tool for the creation and development of Web sites. Many who have little or no experience in the area of Web design have found this software to be easy and fun to use.

The following pages describe several features that make Microsoft PowerPoint a practical tool for Web site creation.

Visual Orientation

First and foremost, Microsoft PowerPoint is a highly visually oriented piece of software, especially with regard to the design process. Pictures, text, colors, and backgrounds can be manipulated and arranged by simply using the mouse, rather than struggling with often-complex HTML code. E. David Ladd, in *Teaching Matters*, the monthly newsletter published by Wayne State University, strongly encourages the use of Microsoft PowerPoint as a tool to reach visual learners (2). Because this software is an effective tool for connecting with students who can be categorized as visual learners, it can create an environment to dramatically enhance learning.

This software also produces visually appealing Web sites. Its colors, images, exciting backgrounds, and multimedia components tend to draw visitors again and again. This is good news for educators who utilize this software; a majority of their site's visitors are their students.

Interchangeable Formats

Microsoft PowerPoint also enables the user to save a project as both a standard presentation and as a Web page. This feature is available in Microsoft PowerPoint versions 97, 2000, and 2002 for those using the Windows Operating System (OS), and versions 98 and 2001 for those using the

Mac OS. This allows for greater flexibility and options within the classroom, as well as online. Furthermore, if a school district has purchased a site license for Microsoft Office, the odds are that Microsoft PowerPoint is included in the package. The same cannot always be said for Microsoft FrontPage, which is the most commonly used Web design software.

Highly Organized

Experienced Web site designers will understand that any file (e.g., a picture) that is used in a Web site needs to be located within a specific folder or directory for it to appear correctly within the Web site. This can become tedious and frustrating for students and teachers alike. Microsoft PowerPoint solves this problem by automatically organizing any files used within the Web site into one organized folder.

Another aspect of Microsoft PowerPoint that aids in organization is the navigational system that is automatically created when the user saves a project as a Web site. This may sound complicated, but actually is simple. The title assigned to each slide in a PowerPoint presentation will be neatly listed in a frame along the left side of each Web page in the Web site. These titles along the side will then become links that a visitor can use to navigate the site. Here is an example:

Microsoft PowerPoint automatically creates a neatly organized system of navigation, eliminating what was traditionally a challenging aspect of Web design—making a Web site navigable.

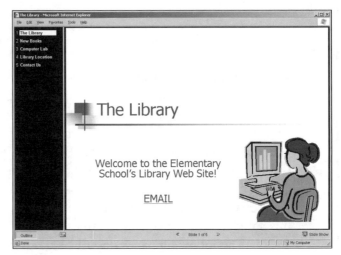

Figure 2.1: The Library Home Page Showing Hyperlinks

Easy to Modify

Teachers who design and use Web sites in the classroom often need to modify or update their site due to a constantly changing learning environment. For many, this has been a complicated process. Files must be accessed and altered in such a manner so that the rest of the site continues to function properly. Many educators have felt that their Web site has become unwieldy and unmanageable, and in frustration, they abandoned their initial efforts to maintain the site.

Microsoft PowerPoint allows users the freedom to easily make changes throughout a presentation or Web site. If a user wishes to add or remove portions of a project, this can be accomplished with a few mouse clicks. Slides can be removed or changed without disturbing the rest of the project. Modifications can be made continually, throughout the life of the Web site, with almost no risk of interfering with the site's proper functioning.

Exciting Background and Color Choices

A variety of preset patterns and color blends make this software appealing to students of all ages (not to mention their teachers!). Users can select from a number of ready-made colors to use with both text and slide backgrounds. These colors can be blended, lightened, or darkened with a click of the mouse. Background textures are also available with this feature, allowing the user to create a background that resembles stone, wood, metal, brick, and other effects. This feature allows library media specialists or teachers to create attractive, professional looking Web sites without needing to resort to lengthy courses in Web design and maintenance.

Creation of Hyperlinks

Microsoft PowerPoint, unlike some other software applications, allows users to seamlessly integrate hyperlinks into their presentation or Web site. Teachers creating a classroom Web site can select objects or text and insert a hyperlink to another Web site, file, or e-mail address quickly and easily. If a teacher has information within a Microsoft Word document or a Microsoft Excel spreadsheet, the file can be linked directly, allowing the viewer to access this file while browsing the Web site. This enables a teacher-created Web site to have a truly global reach, exposing students to the wide variety of resources available online.

Easy Incorporation of Multimedia

With this software, educators can add sound, music, and even video to their presentation or Web site. For example, a music teacher studying the Classical period could add a sound file containing Beethoven's Fifth Symphony to her Web site for students to access online. Because video clips can be added to a Web site or presentation created with Microsoft PowerPoint, a teacher who has filmed his or her students in a speech and debate competition would have the ability to incorporate that video into a Web presentation. With other Web design software on the market today, adding sounds, music, or video to a Web site can be a taxing and confusing experience. However, Microsoft PowerPoint again utilizes a few simple mouse clicks to produce an exciting experience for teachers, students, and parents alike. One cautionary note: When adding multimedia files to a Web site, obtain permission before using copyrighted media.

The Ability to Animate Text and Images

An exciting capability that Microsoft PowerPoint offers is the ability to animate text, images, and even slides. By selecting specific text or images and following a few easy directions, users can add eye-catching animation to their Web presentation. This dynamic feature will capture the attention of students who desperately need motivation.

User Friendly

One of the most attractive aspects of Microsoft PowerPoint as a Web design tool is the help that it affords users who may be new to the software. Depending upon user preference, a variety of help options and tutorials are available within the application itself. An "Office Assistant" is available to assist the user with almost any request. It's like having access to a personal administrative assistant.

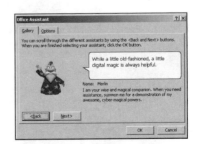

Figure 2.2: Microsoft Office Assistant

Users can simply click on the Office Assistant and ask a question. The assistant will create a space for the user to type the question, then will search for an answer. This user-friendly aspect of Microsoft PowerPoint makes it an excellent application for purposes of educational Web design, and as we will see later, electronic portfolio creation.

Library Media Connection

Library media specialists tend to be familiar with the technological resources available within the school district. Take the time needed to learn the process outlined in this book. Once you feel comfortable using the software, organize professional development workshops for faculty members who are interested in integrating instructional technology, such as Web design, into the classroom. Library media specialists and teachers can collaborate to discover unique ways of integrating technology into the curriculum.

Mini Glossary

HTML	Hypertext Markup Language—a programming language used for creating Web pages.
Hyperlink or Link	A means of connecting one Web page with another, so that when selected, the related Web page will appear.
Operating System (OS)	The software on your computer that controls its basic functioning.
Web Editor	A type of software used for designing and editing Web pages.

Chapter 3

Getting Started

A journey of a thousand miles begins with
a single step.—Lao Tzu

Sometimes starting a project is the most difficult part. By now, you probably have some ideas swirling around in your head—thoughts about ways in which you could use a Web site in conjunction with your classroom activities. Harness that. Don't let it go. Take the next step, and translate your great ideas into actions. Designing a Web site can be enjoyable and not as difficult as you once imagined, thanks to Microsoft PowerPoint.

Step One: Do You Have the Right Hardware?

The first thing you need to look at before you begin the process of Web design is the equipment you have available at your school, library, or home. Has your computer been purchased sometime in the past three years? If so, then you probably have a computer that will be able to handle the necessary tasks. If your computer is three or more years old, then you may want to consider purchasing a new machine or upgrading its components. Older machines can be used if necessary, but the Web design experience will be far more enjoyable if your computer hardware is current. The chart in Figure 3.1 shows the minimum requirements necessary to successfully complete the activities discussed in this book.

Newer computers, with faster processing speeds, can greatly facilitate the Web design process.

Specifications	Recommended
Hard Drive	6 Gigabytes (GB)
RAM	64 Megabytes (MB)
Processor	300 Megahertz (MHz)

Figure 3.1: Recommended Computer Specifications

Step Two: What Kind of Computer Do You Have?

Is your computer a Mac (Macintosh) or a PC (Personal Computer)? The process we will be following is applicable for both Mac and PC machines, but you do need to be aware of this difference. For the most part, the steps used to create Web sites and portfolios using Microsoft

PowerPoint will be the same for both Macs and PCs. However, in some situations, there may be significant differences. Because many school districts purchase both Mac and PC computers, subtle differences between the two platforms will be noted in this book.

Step Three: Do You Have the Right Software?

Find out if you have Microsoft PowerPoint installed on your computer. Typically, Microsoft PowerPoint comes bundled with the Microsoft Office software package. If you find that you do not have Microsoft PowerPoint, you may want to speak with your technology coordinator to inquire about procuring a "site license" for this particular software. A site license allows a software product to be installed on multiple machines owned by the school district. However, if this is not a viable option, you may want to purchase a copy of Microsoft PowerPoint and install the software on your home computer. The software is relatively inexpensive, especially when compared with other software products.

You will also need the correct version of Microsoft PowerPoint, a version that has the capability to transform your presentation into a Web site. This feature is offered in PowerPoint 97, 2000, and 2002 (contained within the Office XP package) for those using the Windows OS, and PowerPoint 98 and 2001 for those using the Mac OS. More recent software will make your Web design experience much easier.

Step Four: Do You Have Internet Access?

This may sound like a basic question, but due to funding shortages, some schools are still without access to the World Wide Web. Check with a library media specialist to find out if your computer is connected to the Internet. At home, you have many choices for Internet Service Providers (ISPs). Look in the Yellow Pages section of your local phone book under "Internet" to find the names and contact information of the ISPs in your area. The ability to connect to the Internet will be vital in order to complete your Web site project.

The speed of an Internet connection can also play an important part, especially when you begin uploading your Web files. The best connections are those that are termed "high-speed." These would include cable, T1, T3, ISDN, or DSL connections. These are usually available from most large ISPs. High-speed Internet access allows a user to remain connected to the Internet at all times without purchasing a second phone line.

Many ISPs offer "dial-up" connections. This type of connection will use local phone lines to access the Internet. Both high-speed and dial-up connections are acceptable for completing the projects within this book, but the faster your Internet connection, the fewer aggravations you will encounter. Library media specialists can further this endeavor by informing faculty as to what kind of Internet connection the school uses. You can also contact your local ISP for more information about plans available in your region.

Step Five: What Is the Purpose of the Web Site?

Before the site can be designed, its purpose must be determined. In Chapter 1, we discussed many different types of Web sites and how they can be used to enhance and reinforce learning. It is often beneficial to brainstorm and record ideas as they materialize. Think about your own curriculum, classroom, or library projects. Which type of Web site would be the best fit for your

Web Site Pre-Design Information	
Type (circle one): Informational Web Portal WebQuest Virtual Field Trip Photo Gallery Topical	
Topic:	
National/State/District Standards Addressed:	
Title of Site:	
Home Page Content:	**Pictures/Media:**
Web Page 1 Title/Content	**Pictures/Media:**
Web Page 2 Title/Content	**Pictures/Media:**
Web Page 3 Title/Content	**Pictures/Media:**

Figure 3.2: Web Site Pre-Design Information Form

course and your students? The library media specialist can further this process, acting as an instructional partner by identifying student needs and ways in which a Web site can be used to meet curriculum standards. By completing the form in Figure 3.2, the focus of your Web site will become more apparent.

Points to Keep in Mind

- The title of the site should relate directly to its stated purpose or topic. This will ensure that visitors to the site will immediately understand what content will be presented. The site's title should be something catchy and creative, and accurately reflect its content.
- Remember that all Web sites begin with a home page that summarizes the purpose of the site and captures attention with pictures or other media. The home page also contains hyperlinks to the other Web pages or sub pages contained within the Web site. It is important to establish the overall purpose or topic of the Web site before the design process is underway. This step will provide focus and clarity to your work.

■ The content specific to each Web page contained within the greater Web site should be carefully planned as well. What should be the topic of each Web page or sub page? If the title of the Web site is "Our Galaxy," then a possible topic for a Web page within the site might be "solar systems." Another Web page topic within this hypothetical Web site could be "quasars." If the topic and subtopics of the Web site are thoughtfully laid out before the site design begins, the site will be more coherent and easier to navigate.

Library Media Connection

To procure the technology necessary to make Web site creation a reality in the school system, library media specialists and teachers will need to work closely together. Library media specialists can help to further the cause of technological integration in the school and classroom in the following ways:

■ Serve in a leadership role to model the integration of technology in instruction.
■ Collaborate with teachers to develop technology rich lessons and units.
■ Find and purchase appropriate hardware and software.
■ Procure Universal Service Fund or E-Rate funding. (Every school in the nation is eligible to receive technology funding from the Universal Service Fund. For more information visit <www.sl.universalservice.org>.)

Teachers are an important part of the technology acquisition process. They can support the library media specialist's efforts to attain the technological resources needed in the following ways:

■ Collaborate with library media specialists to develop technology-rich lessons and projects.
■ Designate a percentage of the funds typically allocated for departmental spending for new computers, monitors, printers, scanners, and so on if a coordinating body for technological expenditures, such as a District Technology Committee, does not exist.
■ Combine funds available within individual classroom budgets with those of other teachers to purchase new technology that can be housed in the library media center for access by all students.

Through close collaboration, teachers and library media specialists can become advocates for propagating new technology throughout their school building. Library media specialists can instruct students and staff in the application of various types of technology to the educational process, and collaborate with teachers to plan, develop, and embed technology components in lessons.

Mini Glossary

Byte A unit of storage on a computer. A byte is 8 bits of data. A kilobyte is roughly 1,000 bytes, a megabyte is 1,000 kilobytes, and a gigabyte is 1,000 megabytes.

Hard Drive The device a computer uses to permanently store information or data.

Hardware The physical parts of a computer that can be touched, such as screen and keyboard.

Megahertz A unit that measures the speed of a processor.

Processor The "brain" of the computer. A device that determines how quickly a computer can process information or data.

RAM Random Access Memory. The memory available to run programs on a computer.

Software An application or set of instructions that tells a computer what to do, usually intangible.

Chapter 4

Adding Slides

You start out to do something—that vague thing called creation.
The beginning strikes awe within you.—Edward Steichen

A uthor Charles Du Bos once exclaimed, "Joy is but the sign that creative emotion is fulfilling its purpose." Many teachers have found that developing their Web site with Microsoft PowerPoint is quite enjoyable, indeed, because it is an effective outlet for the creative impulse. The first step involves adding slides to your presentation. The various slides each serve a slightly different purpose. These slides will eventually become the pages of your Web site, therefore we will discuss them in detail.

Chapter Tips

As you are using Microsoft PowerPoint, keep the following tips in mind:

- If you make a mistake while using the software, simply click on the "Edit" menu and drag down to "Undo." This will undo the last change made to your project. Click "Undo" again to undo the next to last change and so on.
- Save frequently. If you do not save your work every few minutes or so, you risk losing what you have done if your computer freezes or crashes. To save your presentation, click the "File" menu and drag down to "Save." Then select the proper location for your file and give your file a name. The name should be only one word.

Opening Microsoft PowerPoint

The first thing you will need to do is open Microsoft PowerPoint. Look for the PowerPoint icon. If you are using a PC, the Microsoft PowerPoint icon may be located in the "Start" menu or in your "Programs" folder under the heading Microsoft Office. If you are using a Mac, you will probably find the Microsoft PowerPoint icon located under the colored jigsaw menu in the upper right-hand corner of your desktop. When the program opens, it will ask you what type of presentation you would like. Select "Blank Presentation" and then click "OK."

Title Slide

The first slide that should be added to your presentation is known as the "Title Slide." After you have selected "Blank Presentation," you will then be presented with a variety of slide options. Select "Title Slide."

Once you have selected "Title Slide," click "OK." This will take you to the first slide in your presentation. This is the slide that will eventually become the home page, or first page, of your Web site.

You will see a text box that reads "Click to add title." Click there to make the cursor appear. Type the title of your Web site in the space provided. In the text box labeled "Click to add sub-title," type a brief description of your Web site's purpose and content. The title slide is important because, as previously mentioned, it will become the home page of your Web site—the first page visitors to your site see upon accessing the site.

Bulleted List Slide

On many occasions, teachers need to present a list of information about a certain topic. PowerPoint offers a solution to this common need: the "Bulleted List" slide. To create this slide, click on the "Insert" menu, and drag the mouse pointer down to "New Slide." Select the bulleted slide (Figure 4.3).

When you have selected the correct slide option, click "OK." The new slide in Figure 4.4 will appear.

"Click to add title," as indicated by typing the title or topic. Under the title that reads "Click to add text," type the first item on your list. When you press "Enter" (PC) or "Return" (Mac), you will see that a new bullet appears, allowing you to type your next item. In Chapter 8 we will discuss how to animate a bulleted list of items so that each item enters the screen in a special way.

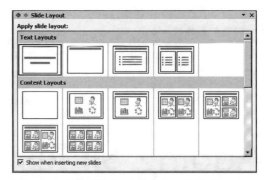

Figure 4.1: Slide Selection Window

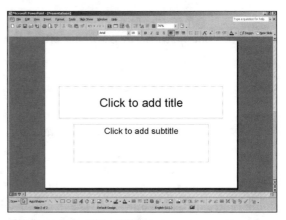

Figure 4.2: Title Slide

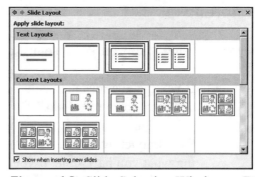

Figure 4.3: Slide Selection Window—Bulleted Slide

Figure 4.4: Bulleted Slide

Table Slide

To effectively present certain kinds of information, most teachers have used a table or a chart. Traditionally, graphic organizers like these have been drawn on chalkboards, glued to poster boards, and so on. PowerPoint provides an attractive alternative to these traditional methods. The "Table Slide" allows a teacher to place information in a table or chart in a way that is easy to manipulate, unlike the aforementioned techniques. To add a "Table Slide" to your presentation, click on the "Insert" menu and drag the mouse pointer down to "New Slide." Select the "Table Slide."

When you click "OK," the slide shown in Figure 4.6 will appear.

As with the other slides, add a title to this table by clicking "Click to add title." Then, double click the section that reads "Double click to add table." You will be presented with the opportunity to choose the number of rows and columns for your table.

After you have made your selection, click "OK." The table you specified will appear in an open Microsoft Word document. Enter the information necessary in each cell of the table. Once you are finished, close the Microsoft Word window. The data you entered will be automatically inserted into your PowerPoint slide. This is an example of how PowerPoint can easily integrate many types of software into the process of creating Web sites and other presentations.

Text & Chart Slide

Graphs and charts are an excellent means to convey data, such as percentages, statistics, and proportions. However, graphs and charts are not always easy to construct and often require fairly complicated calculations. PowerPoint provides a feature that allows users to seamlessly integrate a graph or a chart into their Web site or presentation, known as the "Text & Chart" slide. To add this slide, click on the "Insert" menu, and drag down to "New Slide." Select the "Text & Chart" slide.

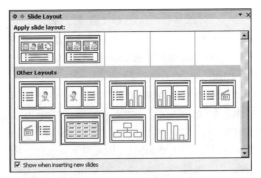

Figure 4.5: Slide Selection Window—Table Slide

Figure 4.6: Table Slide

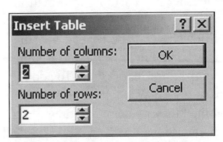

Figure 4.7: Insert Word Table

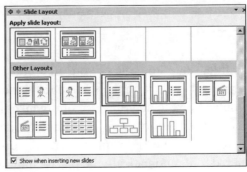

Figure 4.8: Slide Selection Window— Text & Chart Slide

Once you have clicked "OK," a blank slide will appear, as in Figure 4.9.

In the section that reads "Click to add title," type the title of the graph or chart. In the section to the left labeled "Click to add text," type a description of the graph or chart, explaining what is being shown. Finally, double click the section that reads "Double click to add chart." A spreadsheet will appear, allowing the user to enter data that can be organized by means of a graph or a chart. The type of graph or chart can be selected from the many styles available, such as bar graph, circle graph, and others. Once you are finished adding the data, go to the "File" menu, and drag the mouse pointer down to "Quit and return to . . ." This will return you to the slide view. You will see that the data has been arranged in the type of graph or chart you selected.

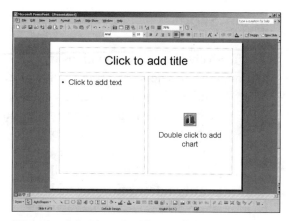

Figure 4.9: Text & Chart Slide

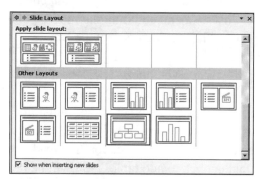

Figure 4.10: Slide Selection Window— Organization Chart

Organization Chart

When a teacher is presenting information that progresses in a step-by-step manner, the use of a flowchart can be beneficial. This option is available in PowerPoint through the "Organization Chart" slide. To add a flow chart to your Web site or presentation, click on the "Insert" menu and drag the mouse pointer down to "New Slide." Select the "Organization Chart" slide:

Once you have clicked "OK," a blank slide will appear, as shown in Figure 4.11.

In the section that reads "Click to add title," enter the title of your flow chart. Then, double click on the section that reads

Figure 4.11: Organization Chart Slide

"Double click to add diagram or organization chart." A new window will appear that allows the user to insert information into the flow chart. Once you are finished inputting the information desired, go to the "File" menu and drag down to "Quit and return to…" The information you entered will automatically be placed into the new flow chart.

Text & Media Clip

Teachers often find the presentation of information via video effective in achieving instructional goals and objectives in the classroom. In a world saturated with television, movies, and video games, video seems to have become our primary means of communication. Many educators feel as though they are in direct competition with this fast paced form of communication. This is where the age-old adage, "If you can't beat them, join them," comes into play. PowerPoint allows a teacher to harness the power of video. The "Text & Media Clip" provides a way in which a short video or audio clip can be inserted into a Web presentation. To add a slide of this type to your presentation, click the "Insert" menu and drag down to "New Slide." Select the "Text & Media Clip" slide:

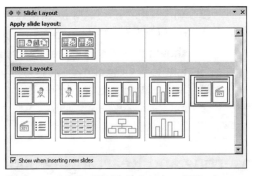

Figure 4.12: Slide Selection Window — Text & Media Clip

When you click "OK," a blank slide will appear as shown in Figure 4.13.

Click the section that reads "Click to add title," and enter the title of the video or audio clip. The section to the left should read "Click to add text." In this section, add a brief description of the media clip. Double click the sentence "Double click to add media clip." A file browser window will open up:

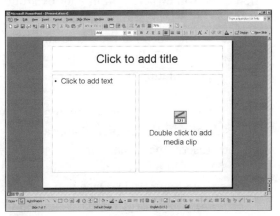

Figure 4.13: Text & Media Clip Slide

If the media clip is located on a CD-ROM, find the CD icon in the file browser window and click it once. If the clip is contained within a folder on your hard drive, double click the folder so that the media clip appears in the file browser window. Whether CD-ROM, floppy disk, or folder, locate the media clip you would like to add to your slide and click "Open." You will notice that the clip has been inserted into your slide. To see how the media clip operates within a slide, click on the "View" menu and drag down to "Slide Show." This

Figure 4.14: File Browser Window — Video

will show the slide as it would appear in a presentation. Click once on the media clip image. This will play the clip. Click again to stop the clip. For another way to incorporate a video or audio file into your Web site, see Chapter 7: Linking to a File.

Considerations

The following are a few points that must be considered before adding video or audio to a PowerPoint slide:

■ Acquiring digital video or audio clips relevant to your curriculum can sometimes be challenging.

- Video that has been recorded onto VHS can be converted into a computer file, provided that the video is original material. Library media specialists and teachers should connect to discuss ways in which video can be edited digitally. It is also important to review copyright issues with a library media specialist or school legal advisor.
- Some Web servers do not support the use of video directly inserted into a Web presentation. Ask your school webmaster or technology coordinator if the server will allow video.

Inserting and Rearranging Slides

Eventually, you may find that you need to insert a new slide somewhere within your existing PowerPoint presentation. If this is the case, click on the "View" menu and drag down to "Slide Sorter." This will allow you to see all of the slides in your presentation in thumbnail form, as shown in Figure 4.15.

Click once either before or after any of the slides displayed. A cursor will appear. Then, click on the "Insert" menu, and drag down to "New Slide." You will be taken through the new slide

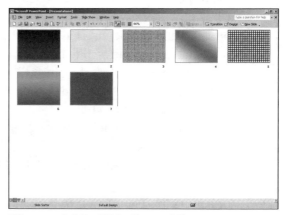

Figure 4.15: Slide Sorter View

choices (see Figure 4.1). Once you click "OK," the new slide will appear where the cursor was.

You may also find that you need to rearrange the slides within your presentation. To do this, click on the "View" menu, and drag down to "Slide Sorter." You again will see the thumbnail display of your slides. Click on the slide you want to move, and drag it to a new location within your presentation. At any time, you may double click on one of the slides shown to edit that particular slide.

PowerPoint provides many different slides that enhance any Web site. These slides will eventually be transformed into the individual pages of your Web site. Some of the most commonly used slides have been discussed throughout this chapter, and more are available. Take some time to experiment with these slides to see how you might make use of them throughout your Web site.

Library Media Connection

Encouragement

School library media specialists often serve as the information and technology expert for the school. Teachers who might be reluctant to use new technology should be encouraged to experiment with Microsoft PowerPoint and the features it offers. Sometimes a little nudge can open up a whole new world of possibilities for teachers and students to explore.

Multimedia

Locate multimedia resources that can be used to enhance an educator-created Web site. Digital video cameras are an excellent way to capture video that is already computer-formatted. If a camera is available, organize a professional development workshop that focuses on training teachers in the use and manipulation of digital video. Two excellent software applications that allow a user to edit digital video are Adobe Premier and iMovie. Finally, seek to acquire CD-ROM resources that offer copyright free, educational video and audio files that can be incorporated into an educational Web site. Digital media files that are in the public domain would also be desirable for a Web project.

Mini Glossary

Presentation   A group of PowerPoint slides arranged to present information.

Slide   A basic part of a PowerPoint presentation.

Text Box   A rectangular area of a PowerPoint slide that contains text.

Chapter 5

Changing the Background

*I saw the angel in the marble and carved
until I set him free.* — M i c h e l a n g e l o

The ability to create colorful and exciting backgrounds for your Web pages is one of the most captivating features of Microsoft PowerPoint as a Web design tool. This software allows you to mix several colors in a variety of ways to produce a stunning and attractive Web site. The creation of such backgrounds will be discussed in some detail throughout this chapter.

Once you have selected one of the slides mentioned in the previous chapter, you can add a colorful background to draw attention to your Web site. *The New York Times* Web site recently ran an article, "The Feng Shui of Schools," which discussed the importance of color to student learning (par. 15). For example, bright colors tend to stimulate brain activity and respiration, while cooler colors promote relaxation. Therefore, the use of color is a key element of an educational Web site.

Basic Colors

To modify the background of a slide, go to the "Format" menu, and drag down to "Background." A new window will pop up, allowing you to select a new background color, as shown in Figure 5.1.

Click once on the white drop down menu to see the colors available. When you see a color you think would be appropriate for your background, click it once. Click "Preview" to see what this color would look like as a background. If you are satisfied with your selection, click "Apply" to apply

Figure 5.1: Background Color Window

this color to the background of your current slide. Click "Apply To All" to apply this color to every slide in your presentation. This feature enables you to create a sense of consistency. This consistency will eventually be carried over when your PowerPoint presentation is transformed into a Web site.

More Colors

If you would like to choose from a wider variety of colors, click on the drop down bar, then click "More Colors." A new window will appear, as in Figure 5.2.

Using the mouse pointer, you can select from a much greater color spectrum. The preview box in the lower right hand corner of this window will show the current background color of your slide next to the new color you have selected with the mouse pointer. If you would like to select from the full color spectrum, adjusting brightness as well, click the tab labeled "Custom." When you are satisfied with your choice, click "OK," which will return you to the window where the new background color can be applied to the current slide or to all slides in the presentation.

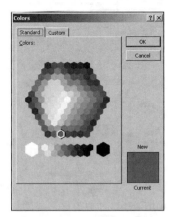

Figure 5.2: Color Selector

Fill Effects

PowerPoint provides eye-catching background effects known as "Fill Effects." Fill Effects allow a user to blend several colors to produce brilliant, almost three-dimensional, background effects. To utilize this feature, click on the "Format" menu, and drag down to "Background." The window as shown in Figure 5.1 will appear. Click on the drop down menu, then click on "Fill Effects." A new window will appear (see Figure 5.3).

Gradient

You will notice below "Colors" that "One-color" is pre-selected. Click the drop down menu underneath "Color 1," and select a color. You can also adjust the brightness of the color selected by adjusting the scale underneath the color menu bar from left to right. The lower left-hand corner of the window contains a section labeled "Shading styles." You can select the direction of shading, and by choosing from the section just to the right entitled "Variants," you can further express your artistic preferences. When you are satisfied with your gradient choices, click "OK." Then click "Apply" or "Apply To All" to see the results.

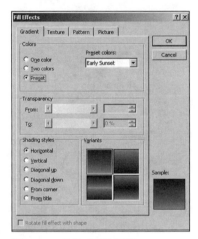

Figure 5.3: Fill Effects—Gradient

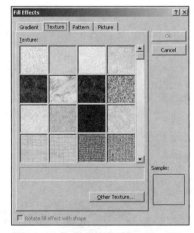

Texture

Another feature of the "Fill Effects" option is the ability to use a specific material texture as a slide background. To experiment with this option, click on the tab labeled "Texture" in the "Fill Effects" window (see Figure 5.3). The window will show texture choices, as shown in Figure 5.4.

Figure 5.4: Fill Effects—Texture

The background texture choices range from brick to wood to bubbles and more. Click on a texture you would like to try as a background, then click "OK." When the background window again appears, click "Apply" or "Apply To All" to see the results. Try different textures to see which ones would be the most compatible with your Web site.

Pattern

The next tab in the "Fill Effects" window is labeled "Pattern." This option permits you to set a particular pattern as a background and adjust its coloration. To try this effect, click on the "Pattern" tab in the "Fill Effects" window. The window should now appear like Figure 5.5.

Choose one of the patterns shown in this window. Try altering the color combinations by changing the foreground. Click on the drop down menu underneath "Foreground." Select a color. Next, click on the drop down menu below "Background." Select a color. Underneath "Sample," you will see a preview of your choice. When you are satisfied with your selection, click "OK." The "Background" window will again appear. Click either "Apply" or "Apply To All" to see the results.

Picture

PowerPoint makes it possible to set a picture or graphic as the background. Click on the "Picture" tab while in the "Fill Effects" window. The window will appear like this as in Figure 5.6.

To choose a picture, click the button labeled "Select Picture." A file browser window will appear (see Figure 5.7).

Locate the picture you would like to set as your background, then click "Insert." In the "Fill Effects" window, click "OK." The picture will then appear as the background of your slide.

The background of a Web page can set the mood for visitors to your site. The backgrounds that can be created through Microsoft PowerPoint are captivating and can be modified to fit the atmosphere of your Web site. The best way to learn which backgrounds work with your particular site is to experiment with different options.

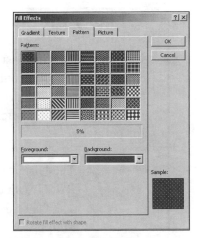

Figure 5.5: Fill Effects — Pattern

Figure 5.6: Fill Effects — Picture

Figure 5.7: File Browser Window

Library Media Connection

Library media specialists can collaborate with teachers by acquiring images related to a teacher's Web site content to incorporate into a Web page background. A variety of CD-ROMs with images and graphics are available from educational distributors. The following Web sites offer either free educational clip art or image CD-ROMs available for purchase:

- The Discovery Channel <http://school.discovery.com/clipart/> (offers CD-ROMs with educational clip art images)
- The Classroom Clipart Sources <http://208.183.128.3/techupdate/classclip.html>
- The School Clipart for Teachers and Kids <http://www.school-clip-art.com/>

Often, students are an excellent resource. Students who have experience in the use of software or layout and design can be invited to volunteer in the library to assist teachers.

Mini Glossary

Window   Rectangular portion of a display being used by a specific program.

Chapter 6

Adding Text

Words are, of course, the most powerful drug
used by mankind. — Rudyard Kipling

Words, as Rudyard Kipling notes, are powerful indeed. Wars have been waged over words. With so much attention being placed on colors and visual effects, neglecting the importance of words to your Web site would be easy. Many visitors complain about an overabundance of text on some Web sites. However, when used properly, text can help to clarify the purpose of a Web page. This chapter deals with the issues surrounding the use of text in your presentation or Web site.

Text Box

Most PowerPoint slides contain text boxes that allow you to enter text. Using the steps outlined in the last chapter, create a new slide. To add text to the new slide, click on the text box once. A blinking cursor should appear inside the text box. If a cursor does not appear within the text box, you may have selected the entire text box, rather than just a cursor point within the text box. If this happens, click once again inside the text box.

If you would like to insert an additional text box, click the "Insert" menu, and drag down to "Text Box." Your mouse pointer should now appear as a cursor. Click and drag your mouse pointer to determine the size and location of the text box. In the same way you entered text into the existing text boxes, you can now do the same with the new text box that has been created. This feature makes adding text to a Web page quick and easy.

Size

The size of your text is an important issue when considering the overall design of each Web page. To change the size of the text you have entered, click once inside the text box. A cursor should appear inside the text box. Using your mouse pointer, highlight the text you wish to modify (see Figure 6.1 on page 48).

Next, click on the "Format" menu, and drag down to "Font." A new window should appear as in Figure 6.2.

Underneath "Size," select a new size for the text you have highlighted, then click "OK." You will immediately see the change in size in the current slide (see Figure 6.3).

If you would like to make further changes to text, repeat the process just outlined.

Font

When adding text to any Web site, it is important to be aware of the text font. Style guidelines suggest that the font should be consistent throughout the Web site. Does this mean that you have to follow the rules? No. The Web site is your creation, but consistent patterns, fonts, and colors throughout your site will create the sense that the Web site has been professionally designed. To change the font, highlight the text you would like to modify, as shown in Figure 6.4 on the following page.

Once the text has been highlighted, click on the "Format" menu, and drag down to "Font." A window will appear like the one in Figure 6.5.

Under "Font," you will see the current font of the high-lighted text. Below the current font, Times, appears a scrolling list of fonts available on your computer. Different computers contain different fonts. The fonts that are common to almost all

Figure 6.1: Text Box — Highlighted Text

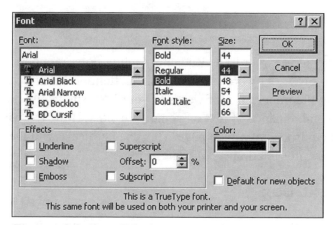

Figure 6.2: Font Window

Figure 6.3: Font Size

computers are "Arial," "Times," and "Chicago." A number of fonts are also available free online. Use a search engine, such as Yahoo! or Google, to locate Web sites that provide fonts. Select a font from the list. For the purposes of this example, we will select the "Arial" font.

You can also change the font style. Under "Font Style," choose a new style for the text you have selected, either Regular, Bold, Italic, or Bold Italic. In this example, we will change the font style to Bold. When you are satisfied with your choices, click "OK." You will notice that the changes take place instantly. as shown in Figure 6.6.

Go back through the preceding steps if you are not pleased with the appearance of the text. Experiment with different fonts and font styles. As educators, we know that the best way to learn is to do. As Confucius proposed, "I hear and I forget. I see and I remember. I do and I understand." Think about the overall look that you are trying to achieve. Which font would best complement your Web site?

Color

The use of color is another critical aspect of effective Web design. Like font and style, the colors used throughout your Web site should also be consistent. To change the text color, highlight the text to be modified, as shown in Figure 6.7 on the following page.

Click on the "Format" menu, and drag down to "Font." A window will appear like the one shown in Figure 6.8.

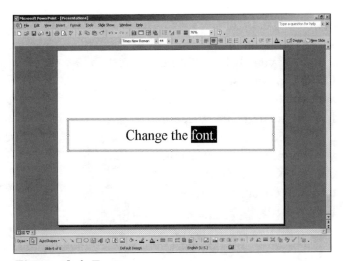

Figure 6.4: Font

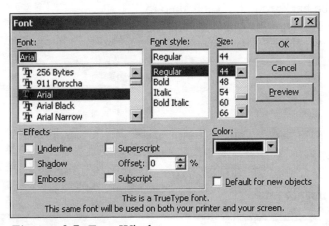

Figure 6.5: Font Window

Figure 6.6: Font Style

Under "Color," you will see the current text color, which in this example is black. To change the color, click on the arrow next to the current text color. You will be presented with a number of color choices, as shown in Figure 6.9.

If you click on "More Colors," a color spectrum will appear, allowing you to choose from a much greater selection of colors (see Figure 5.2). Once you have chosen a new color, click "OK." The changes will be immediately apparent (see Figure 6.10).

In this example, the color red was selected. Try a variety of text colors. When choosing a new color, consider the background of each slide to make sure that the pages in your Web site will be clear and readable.

Figure 6.7: Font Color

Location

The location of the text on each Web page is significant for many reasons. Text should enhance and clarify the purpose of a Web page, not distract from it. Text that overlaps a picture or graphic on your page will often be unreadable. Text that is poorly aligned or runs off the page may cause visitors to become frustrated and leave the Web site. Fortunately, PowerPoint alleviates this problem by neatly arranging most text boxes as observed in Chapter 4.

To rearrange the location of text on the current slide, click once on the text box. The text box itself should become highlighted, without a cursor. If a cursor appears, click somewhere else on the slide, and try again.

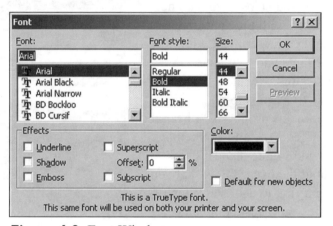

Figure 6.8: Font Window

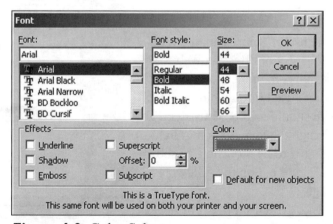

Figure 6.9: Color Selector

Once the text box is highlighted, click and hold the text box, and use your mouse to drag to a new location. PowerPoint allows you to click and drag most objects to new locations, whether images, text boxes, or media items.

No doubt about it, text is an important component in any Web site, educational or otherwise. Take the time to consider how text can be used to explain portions of your site that may require some clarification. Used appropriately, the selection of fonts, colors, and text styles can complement the look and feel of an educational Web site.

Figure 6.10: Font Color

Mini Glossary

Font An assortment of characters all of one style.

Text The words, characters, and numbers utilized in a Web page.

Window Rectangular portion of a display being used by a specific program.

Chapter 7

Adding Hyperlinks

No man is an island. — John Donne

The advent of the Internet in 1969 made possible, for the first time, the direct communication between computers and networks on a vast scale. One of the strengths of the Internet is the vast array of resources and ideas available to the average user. Educators who create a Web site with a focus on a specific topic will almost certainly find other Web sites of similar interest. Through the use of hyperlinks, a Web site can provide access to many other Web sites throughout the World Wide Web. Not only can hyperlinks connect visitors to other Web sites, they can also provide access to files, an e-mail address, and even another page of your Web site. This chapter will explain how to incorporate hyperlinks into your Web site.

Finding Appropriate Web Sites

The first step of the hyperlink process is finding Web sites that are suitable for linking to your site. What is the topic of your Web site? What is the expected age range of your Web site visitors? A search engine is often a good starting point. Try a search engine such as Yahoo!, Excite, or Google. For example, if the topic of your Web site is California, then you would conduct a search using the keyword "California." A listing of Web sites that contain information about California will appear. Carefully browse through the Web sites you would like to consider as links. As information specialists, library media specialists can provide selection criteria and guidance throughout the link selection process. Typically, Web sites with domain names that end in .edu are hosted by educational institutions such as colleges and universities. Domains that end in .gov or .mil are government or military sites. Web sites in these categories often contain reliable information; nevertheless, carefully scrutinize all sites that you link to yours.

Creating a Hyperlink

Through PowerPoint, you can quickly and easily insert a hyperlink into text, photos, or graphics. Use the following steps to add hyperlinks to your Web site.

Inserting into Text

If you would like to insert a hyperlink into a word or group of words, begin by highlighting the text, as shown in Figure 7.1.

Next, click the "Insert" menu, and drag down to "Hyperlink." A new window will appear that allows you to specify where you want the hyperlink to take the Web site visitor (see Figure 7.2).

Below "Link to File or URL," type or "copy and paste" in the space provided the URL or Web address of the Web site to which you would like to link. Once you have entered the URL, click "OK." You will notice that the text you have highlighted has changed as shown in Figure 7.3.

Now, when visitors to your Web site click on the word or words you have chosen, they will be immediately taken to the Web site to which you have linked.

Inserting into Photos or Graphics

To insert a hyperlink into a photo or graphic, click once on the image (directions for inserting an image into a slide can be found in Chapter 8). You will notice that the image now appears with sizing handles as shown in Figure 7.4 on the following page.

For directions about resizing an image using sizing handles, refer to Chapter 8.

Figure 7.1: Inserting a Hyperlink

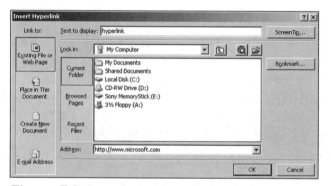

Figure 7.2: Inserting a Hyperlink Window

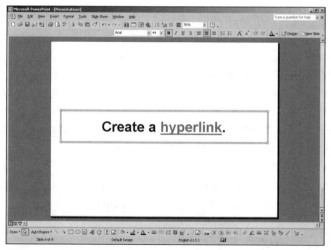

Figure 7.3: Hyperlink Text

Click the "Insert" menu, and drag down to "Hyperlink." A new window will appear (see Figure 7.2). Below "Link to File or URL" in the space provided, type the URL of the Web site to which you would like to link. Once you have entered the URL, click "OK." Now, when visitors to your Web site click the image, they will be immediately taken to the specified Web site.

Linking to a File

With this software, you are able to link not only to another Web site, but to another file, such as a Microsoft Word document, a Microsoft Excel file, or a video file. To link to a file, you should first make sure that the file in question has been saved or relocated to the folder or directory where your PowerPoint presentation has been saved. Next, highlight the text or picture that will contain the link. Then, click the "Insert" menu, and drag down to "Hyperlink." A new window will appear allowing you to specify the hyperlink path (see Figure 7.2). Underneath "Link to File or URL," click once on the "Select" button if you are using a Mac, or "Browse" if you are using a "PC." A file-browsing window will appear, enabling you to search for the file to which you wish to link (see Figure 7.5).

Click once on the correct file, then click "OK." Now, when visitors to your Web site click on this link, they will be given the option to either save the specified file or open it. This is an excellent way to display a lengthy text file, such as student essays, project guidelines, video, and audio files, without taking up space on your Web site.

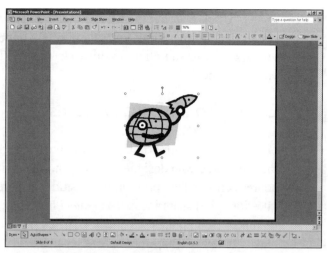

Figure 7.4: Hyperlink Image

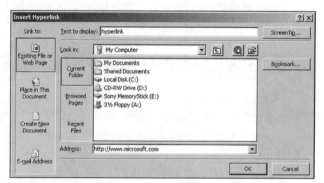

Figure 7.5: File Browser Window

Linking to Another Slide

PowerPoint will also permit you to link one slide to another. When the slide presentation is finally converted to a Web site, this action will link one Web page to another. For example, a teacher who develops a Web site about the history and culture of Japan could directly link pages of relevant information. A Web page that focuses on the Samurai tradition might reference (using a hyperlink) another Web page within the same Web site that provides an overview of the formation of the feudal system in Japan.

To create a hyperlink to another slide in the same presentation, highlight the text or image to be linked (see Figures 7.3 and 7.4). Click the "Insert" menu, and drag down to "Hyperlink." The hyperlink options window will appear (see Figure 7.2). Below "Named location in file," click the "Select" button. You will see the titles of the slides you have created up to this point as shown in Figure 7.6.

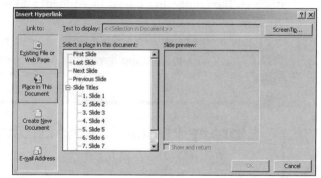

Figure 7.6: Hyperlink to Slide

Click once on the title of the slide to which you would like to create a hyperlink, then click "OK." A hyperlink inserted into text appears in a different color (see Figure 7.3). When visitors to your site click on this link, they will be immediately taken to the slide (Web page) you have specified.

Linking to an E-mail Address

One of the most important purposes of a Web site is to provide a means of communication between the individual who designed the site and the visitor to the site. Creating a hyperlink to an e-mail address creates the opportunity for students, parents, and teachers to exchange information, ask questions, and share ideas. To create a hyperlink to an e-mail address, highlight the text or image to be linked (see Figures 7.3 and 7.4). Click on the "Insert" menu, and drag down to "Hyperlink." A new window will appear where you can specify where the hyperlink should take the Web site visitor (see Figure 7.2). Underneath "Link to File or URL," type "mailto:" immediately followed by the e-mail address in the space provided (mailto:educator@e-mail.com). When visitors to your Web site click on this hyperlink, they will be able to send e-mail to the address specified.

Changing Hyperlink Color

Sometimes when a hyperlink is inserted into text, the color does not always fit into the color scheme you intend for the Web site. Fortunately, this is a relatively easy problem to correct. Simply click the "Format" menu, and drag down to "Slide Color Scheme." A new window entitled "Color Scheme" will appear. Click once on the tab that is labeled "Custom", as in Figure 7.7.

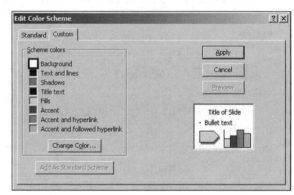

Figure 7.7: Slide Color Scheme

To change the hyperlink color, click once on the color-square next to "Accent and hyperlink." Then, click the "Change Color" button. A color spectrum will appear that allows the user to select a new hyperlink color (see Figure 5.2). Once you have selected a color that will fit with the look and feel of your Web site, click "OK." This will change the hyperlink color for the current slide.

Library Media Connection

Collaborate with teachers and technology coordinators to create a directory of Web sites that are appropriate for educational use. Organize the directory into subject categories so that Web sites will be easy to locate, then make this directory accessible to both teachers and students. The development of an educational Web site directory will require faculty members to search through various Web sites.

Many school districts maintain an "Acceptable Use Policy" with regards to teacher and student use of the Internet that specifies proper use, rules, and regulations for accessing the Internet at school. If the district does not have such a policy in place, library media specialists, teachers, and administrators should work to develop one.

Mini Glossary

Hyperlink or Link A means of connecting one Web page with another, so that when selected, the related Web page will appear.

Internet A worldwide network connecting millions of computers for communications purposes.

Keywords Words or phrases entered into a search field of a search engine to locate relevant Web sites.

Search Engine A tool on the Web that allows a user to search for Web sites based on certain criteria.

World Wide Web or WWW or Web An interface for the Internet, made up of computers that provide access to documents that further provide access to other documents, multimedia files, and Web pages.

Chapter 8

Adding Images, Logos, and Animation

A picture is worth a thousand words. — Napoleon

Think back to the days when you were a child, sitting in a desk, facing your classroom teacher. For some of us, that is quite a stretch! Perhaps your teacher was discussing a foreign land, an aquatic animal, or another planet. What aroused your interest in that lesson? Was it the words that were read? Was it the words that were spoken? Or... could it have been a picture that was displayed for the class? If you were then like a majority of students today, the picture would probably have provided you with the most information. It is important to integrate images into educational Web sites because more and more students are visually wired (Mustapha). This chapter will discuss the basics of adding images to your Web site, as well as creating visually stimulating logos using Microsoft WordArt®.

Inserting Clip Art

PowerPoint offers a convenient feature that makes adding images to your site quick and easy. Within this software exists a gallery of ready-made clip art images that cover a variety of topics. To insert a clip art image into a Web page, click on the "Insert" menu, and drag down to "Picture." A new menu will appear to the right of "Picture," as shown in Figure 8.1.

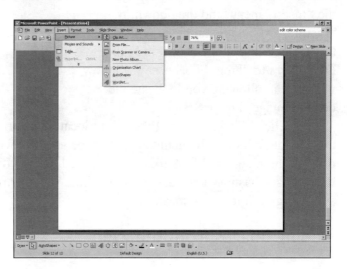

Figure 8.1: Inserting a Picture

Drag across to "Clip Art" and release. A new window will appear, as shown in Figure 8.2.

You will observe that various categories are listed in a scrolling section to the left, while clip art graphics within each category are showcased in the scrolling section in the middle. Click a category to see the clip art it contains. Browse through the clip art files to find an image that fits the topic of the Web page. Once you have found the right clip art graphic, click it once, then click "Insert." This will add the clip art image to your current slide. To move the image to a new position, simply click and drag the image to the desired location. If the image is positioned over the top of text or another image, you can correct this by right clicking on the image and dragging down to "Arrange" if you are using a PC. Select "Send Backward" to move the image back one layer. Repeat the process if necessary. If you are using a Mac, click the image while pressing the "CTRL" key. A menu will appear. Drag down to "Order," and select "Send Backward." Repeat the steps if necessary. More exact modifications can be made to the image; these will be discussed in detail later in this chapter.

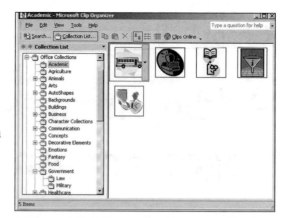

Figure 8.2: Microsoft Clip Art Gallery

Inserting Images from a File

If you have a file of photos, graphics, or other images you would like to insert into your Web site, you can accomplish this through a few easy-to-follow steps. Click the "Insert" menu, and drag down to "Picture." An additional menu will appear to the side like the one shown in Figure 8.1. Drag down to "From File." A new window will appear, allowing you to locate the desired image (Figure 8.3).

Figure 8.3: File Browser Window

Click "Find File" or "Browse" to locate the correct Image file. Once you have located the file, click it once. It should appear in the small preview window. This will give you an idea of what the image will look like once inserted. Click "Insert." You should see that the image you have chosen has now been added to the slide. You may rearrange the image position by clicking and dragging it to a new location.

Adding Images from the Web

The World Wide Web is comprised of billions of Web pages dealing with literally every topic known to humankind. While browsing through this mass of information, you may have come across photos, graphics, or other images that you feel would enhance your Web site. With PowerPoint you can quickly and easily harvest pictures from another Web site to add to your own.

When you discover an image on another Web page that you would like to incorporate into your own, the first step is to obtain permission. Look for an e-mail address or other contact information on the Web site containing the image. Ask the webmaster for permission to use the image in your Web site. Usually, webmasters will agree to let you use the image if you inform them that your Web site will be used for educational purposes. Many who have designed Web sites have neglected to ask a webmaster for permission to use an image on their site. Asking for and obtaining permission is the ethical and legal step to take, as well as being a courteous gesture.

If the webmaster authorizes the use of the image on your Web site via e-mail, keep a copy of that e-mail for your records. Below the image, reference the Web site from where the image was originally found. Library media specialists and teachers should discuss legal issues surrounding copyrights and intellectual property. Give credit where credit is due.

Once you have obtained permissions, mouse over the image. If you are using a Mac, click and hold until a menu appears. Drag down to "Copy Image." If you are using a PC, right click on the image. When the menu appears, drag down to "Copy." When you have selected the slide in which you would like to add the image, click on the "Edit" menu, and drag down to "Paste." The image should appear on the slide. You may rearrange the image on the page by clicking and dragging to a new location.

Altering Image Size

When an image is inserted into a slide, it may not be the correct size. This is an easy problem to remedy. To adjust the size, click once on the image. The image should now appear with sizing handles, as shown in Figure 8.4.

Move the mouse over any of the four corner sizing handles. Notice the mouse pointer immediately changes into a bi-directional arrow. Click, hold, and drag. You will see that the image size changes as you

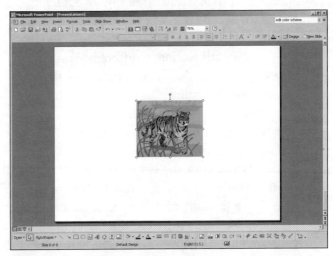

Figure 8.4: Altering Image Size

move the mouse. Select a size that is appropriate for your Web page, then release the mouse. The image will now appear in the correct size. You may alter the image size using the side sizing handles, but the scale will be altered, leaving a distorted image. If you are unsatisfied with a change, simply click on the "Edit" menu, and drag down to "Undo." This will reverse the last change. Experiment with the image-sizing feature until you have achieved the look you want. As with many things in life, trial and error is often one of the best ways to learn a new skill.

Altering Image Appearance

To modify the appearance of the image, click once on the image. You should now see the sizing handles.

Figure 8.5: Picture Toolbar

Next, click on the "View" menu. Drag down to "Toolbars," and drag across to "Picture." A toolbar should appear, as shown in Figure 8.5.

If this toolbar does not appear, it may already be located in the PowerPoint tools. If this is the case, scan the screen for a toolbar that looks like the one in Figure 8.5.

Using the buttons available on this toolbar, you can alter the brightness and contrast of the image. Move the mouse over each button. As you hover the mouse pointer over each button, a screen tip will appear, informing you of the purpose of the button. Experiment with the buttons. If you are unsatisfied with a change, simply click on the "Edit" menu, and drag down to "Undo." This will reverse the last change.

Using WordArt to Create a Logo

A fancy logo or title can add a great deal to any Web site, drawing the attention of site visitors. WordArt is a feature of PowerPoint that permits you to effortlessly create attractive and professional-looking logos for a Web page. To experiment with WordArt, click on the "Insert" menu, and drag down to "Picture." A new menu will appear next to "Picture" (see Figure 8.1). Drag across to "WordArt." A new window will appear (Figure 8.6).

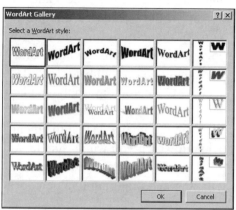

Figure 8.6: WordArt Gallery

You will see many different WordArt styles. Select one that will complement the Web site you are designing. Once you have chosen a style, click it once, then click "OK." A new window will appear that allows you to enter the logo text, as shown in Figure 8.7.

If you click the bar under "Font," you will see that you are able to change the font of the logo. Try a few different fonts until you find one that goes well with the overall look and feel of your Web page. Below "Size," you will see a menu bar that allows you to increase or decrease the text size. The buttons to the right give you the ability to bold or italicize the text. Once you are ready, click "OK" to see your text displayed as WordArt, as in Figure 8.8.

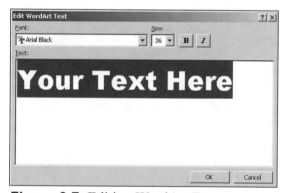

Figure 8.7: Editing WordArt Text

To adjust the color of the WordArt logo, click the logo once, then click the "View" menu, and drag down to "Toolbars." A new menu will appear next to "Toolbars." Drag down to "WordArt." This will cause the WordArt toolbar to appear (see Figure 8.9).

Text

To change the text of the logo, click "Edit Text." The text box will again appear, allowing you to change the text (see Figure 8.7).

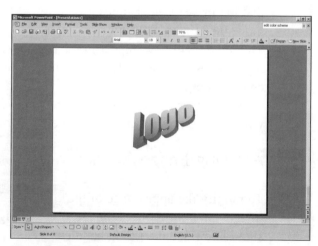

Figure 8.8: WordArt

Style

If you would like to select a new WordArt style, click the tilted "A." The WordArt style window will again appear (see Figure 8.6).

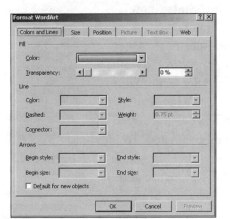

Figure 8.9: WordArt Toolbar

Color

If you would like to change the color scheme of your logo, click the paint bucket and brush icon. A new window will appear (Figure 8.10).

Under "Fill," you will notice a color bar menu. Click this bar once to select a new fill color for your WordArt logo. Below "Line," you will see another color bar. Click this bar once to select a new color for the outline of your WordArt logo. Once you are finished, click "OK" to see the changes.

Figure 8.10: Format WordArt

Shape

If you would like to change the shape of your WordArt logo, click the "ABC" button located on the WordArt toolbar. A shape menu will appear (Figure 8.11).

These shapes reflect the shape your WordArt logo will take if chosen. Find one that works for you, and click it once. You should notice that your logo assumes the new shape assigned to it.

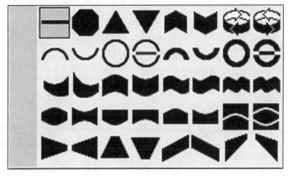

Figure 8.11: WordArt Shape

Experiment with the image and image editing possibilities afforded by this software. Have fun trying different colors, shapes, outlines, sizes, and fonts. Consider the excitement this software will generate among your students when they begin adding and editing images for their individual Web portfolios!

Animation

Human vision is based on motion. Your eyes are constantly moving to process the visual information they are receiving. Motion draws attention. A baby's eyes will follow a moving object, while one that is still attracts little notice. Using Microsoft PowerPoint, it is possible to incorporate a variety of animation effects into a Web presentation. From a word flying across the screen to an image materializing as if from thin air, animation can add a great deal to any Web site.

Animating Text

Often, animation effects are used to focus student attention on a particular word, phrase, or sentence. To animate any text box on a PowerPoint slide, click the text box to highlight it, as shown in Figure 8.12 on page 64.

Once you have selected the text box, click the "Slide Show" menu, and drag down to "Preset Animation" if you are using a Mac. If you are using a PC, click the "Slide Show" menu, and drag down to "Animation Schemes." A new menu will appear to the right, listing the available animation features (e.g., Flying, Camera, and Laser Text). Click any of the animation effects listed. To view the animation effect in action, click the "View" menu, and drag down to "Slide Show." Once the slide show appears, click to activate the animation effect. Press the "Esc" button on the keyboard to return to the "Slide" view. These animation effects can be used with bulleted lists as well. Experiment with the different effects offered. Have fun!

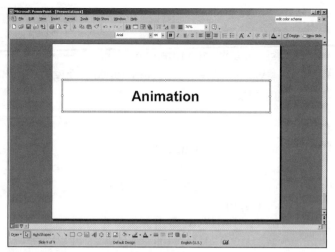

Figure 8.12: Animating Text

Animating Images

Images add color and life to what would otherwise be a text only Web site. The dynamic ani-

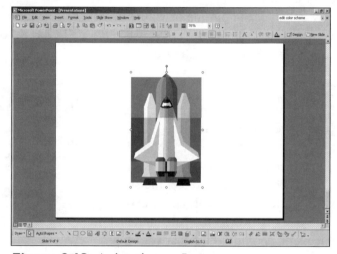

Figure 8.13: Animating an Image

mations applied to text can be further applied to images. To perform this function, click the image once to select it (Figure 8.13).

Once you have selected the image, click on the "Slide Show" menu, and drag down to "Preset Animation" or "Animation Scheme." A new menu will appear to the right, listing the image animation features (e.g., Drive-in, Wipe Right, and Dissolve). Click any of the animation effects listed. If you would like to see the animation effect in action, click the "View" menu, and drag down to "Slide Show." Once the slide show appears, click to activate the animation effect. Press the "Esc" button on the keyboard to return to the "Slide" view. Try using different animation effects to see which one looks best with the image you have selected.

Slide Transition Effects

Not only does PowerPoint let you animate text and images, it also allows you to animate entire slides. This provides for exciting transitions from one slide to the next. Moreover, you can add sound effects to the slide transition. To create a slide transition effect, click on the "Slide Show" menu, and drag down to "Slide Transition." A new window will appear, as shown in Figure 8.14 on the following page.

Click the bar menu labeled "No Transition." A list of transition effects will appear. Below the "Sound" heading, click the bar labeled "No Sound" to see sounds that can accompany the selected slide transition. Select an effect, then click the "Apply" button to apply the effect to the current slide. Or, if you would like to apply the effect to all of the slides in the presentation, click "Apply to all." If you would like to see the slide transition effect, click the "View" menu, and drag down to "Slide Show." Once the slide show appears, click once to activate the slide transition. Press

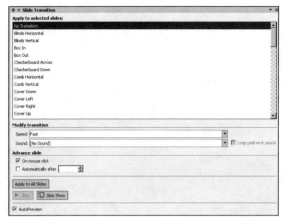

Figure 8.14: Slide Transition Window

the "Esc" button on the keyboard to return to the "Slide" view. Experiment with different slide transitions to find out which one you want to use. Make sure the volume on your computer is turned up to hear the sound effects you have added! One cautionary note: Some Web browsers may not support animation effects created with Microsoft PowerPoint.

Library Media Connection

Many wonderful CD-ROM image collections are available through educational catalogs and distributors (see Library Media Connection in Chapter 5). Similar to a Web site directory, an image directory can also be developed. Explore Web sites and CD-ROMs for images that can be organized into subject categories. This will be of great help to teachers who are in the process of designing a Web site, and students who are creating a Web portfolio. However, teachers and students should be reminded that they need permission from the owner of a Web site prior to using a picture from that site. Coordinate a professional development workshop that addresses legal issues and the Internet, as well as the school or district copyright policy. Visit <www.Webreference.com/internet/legal.html> to learn more.

Mini Glossary

Sizing Handles The tiny squares that appear on each corner and each side of an image when the user clicks on it once. The sizing handles allow a user to adjust image size.

Slide Transition The movement from one PowerPoint slide to the next.

Webmaster The person who manages a Web site; the administrative contact.

Chapter 9

Web Hosting and Publishing Your Web Site

There's no place like home. — Dorothy in *The Wizard of Oz*

Now that you are finished with the Web design phase, consider how others will be able to access your Web site. You will need to load the files related to your Web site on a Web server to make them available through the Internet. When you read the words "Web server," did your eyes begin to glaze over? When they hear such techno-jargon, many people immediately begin to lose interest, often because they assume that the meanings of those words are confusing and too technical. This chapter will attempt to clarify certain computer-related concepts so you can successfully publish your Web site to the World Wide Web.

Converting a PowerPoint Presentation to a Web Site

Before you convert your PowerPoint presentation to a Web site, save it as a presentation. If you have not already done so, click the "File" menu, and drag down to "Save." A window like the one shown in Figure 9.1 will appear.

Below "Save As," type a name for your presentation. The name should reflect the purpose of the Web site. For example, if your Web site focuses on the formation of volcanoes along the Pacific Rim, you might want to name your presentation "volcanoes." By saving your work as a presentation, you will be able to make changes to

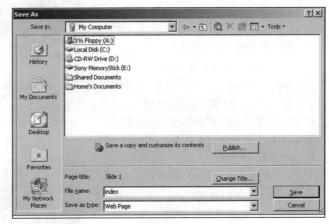

Figure 9.1: File Save Window

your Web site even after it has been uploaded to a Web server.

Once you have saved your PowerPoint presentation and are ready to convert it into a Web site, click once again on the "File" menu. Next, drag down to "Save As." A new window will appear (see Figure 9.1). Next to "Save File as Type" select "Web Page." Click the "Change Title… " button to give your site a title (e.g., "Pacific Rim Volcanoes"). Below "Save As," enter the filename for the Web site you have created. You should name the file "index.html." This will allow for easier access to your Web site once it is published. The top of the window will display the name of the folder or directory where the Web site will be located. Use the menu bar at the top to select the proper location for your Web site. Once you are finished, click "Save." If you look in the folder or directory where you saved your Web site, you should notice that there is now an HTML file labeled "index.html" and a folder labeled "index_files." The "index_files" folder contains all of the files that make up your Web site.

Variation

MacIntosh versions of Microsoft PowerPoint will convert a presentation to a Web site in a slightly different manner. If you follow the steps described previously, you might notice that next to "Save File as Type," the option to save your presentation as a "Web Page" or "Web Site" is not available. Instead, you should click on the "File" menu, and drag down to "Save As HTML." A new window will appear, as shown in Figure 9.2.

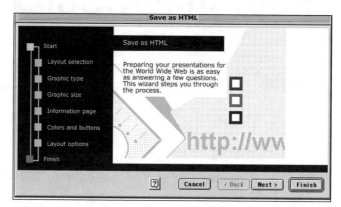

Figure 9.2: Save as HTML Wizard

This window is known as a "wizard" because it takes you step-by-step through a process. Once you have read the introduction, click "Next." The next step will be to select a Web page style. You should select the "Browser frames" option as shown in Figure 9.3.

Once you have made your selection, click "Next." For the purposes of this project, you will want to click "Finish." You will then be prompted to select a destination folder for your Web site (Figure 9.4).

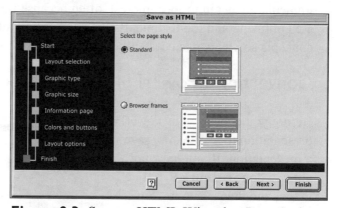

Figure 9.3: Save as HTML Wizard—Page Style

Click "Select" and choose a destination folder for your Web site. Once you have done so, click "Next." Then click "Finish." Your Web site will now be located in the folder or directory specified. Once you open the specified folder, you will need to look for an HTML file labeled "index.htm." This is the home page of your Web site.

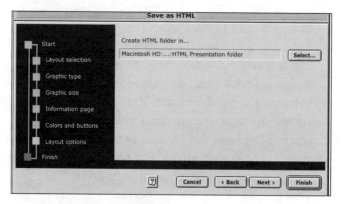

Figure 9.4: Save as HTML Wizard—File Destination Folder

Using the School's Web Server

A number of schools maintain a Web site that provides at least some basic information about the district, community, and so on. This Web site must be hosted on a server so that people can access it through the Internet. Many schools have opted to run their own server rather than lease server space from an outside vendor. This school-operated server is probably the best Web hosting option for your Web site.

PROS

- Hosting your Web site on the school's Web server is free.
- The school will not require you to display annoying pop up advertisements on your Web site, as will many free Web hosting companies.

CONS

- You may be assigned a domain name, or Web address, that is often lengthy and difficult to remember.

Free Web Hosting

If your school does not provide a Web server to host your Web site or does not permit teachers to access its server, other alternatives do exist. One such alternative is free Web hosting. Many companies offer their Web server free of charge. Does this sound too good to be true? Well, there is a catch. In exchange for the server space they provide for your Web site, they most often require you to display an advertisement on your Web site. This may range from a banner ad at the top or bottom of each Web page, to a pop up advertisement that appears as soon as a visitor loads your page. If you use a search engine such as Yahoo! or Google, you can simply conduct a Web search for "free Web hosting." Typically, you will discover hundreds of organizations willing to offer free Web hosting in exchange for some sort of advertising rights.

Be cautious when choosing a free Web host because you will usually have little control over what kinds of advertisements are displayed on your Web site. Some educationally related Web hosts will offer free Web hosting for educators or educational Web sites. If you are a classroom teacher, consult your library media specialist before selecting a free Web host. Library media specialists will search to find sites that are most appropriate. Some school district Internet policies specifically prohibit the use of free Web hosting services by students and faculty.

PROS

- This type of Web hosting is free of charge.
- Many options are available.

CONS

- You must allow pop up advertisements to be displayed on your Web site.
- You may be assigned a domain name that is lengthy and difficult to remember.

Paid Web Hosting

Another Web hosting option is what is frequently referred to as "paid Web hosting." Paid Web hosting means that users (e.g., the library media specialist) pay a company to provide Web server space for their Web site. Usually, a fee is paid on a monthly or annual basis, and can range anywhere from $5 to $100 or more per month. However, the average cost should be no more than $10 per month for hosting the type of Web site we have been discussing throughout this book. The benefit of paid Web hosting compared to free Web hosting is that you are not required to display advertisements on your Web site. Most paid Web hosts will require that you agree to at least one year of service.

PROS

- Your Web site will be free of advertisements.
- Many Web hosts will include domain name (URL) registration in their fee or provide such services at a low price. This will enable you to select your own Web address (i.e., www.mywebsitename.com).

CONS

- You must pay a monthly or annual fee with this type of hosting.

Uploading Options

Once you have decided which type of Web server to utilize, the next item to consider is how to upload or send the Web site you have just created to its new home on the Web server. One option is the school's Web server, which may have an established method for uploading files to the server. Take time to discuss upload options with your school's library media specialist, or school or district technology coordinator.

FTP

FTP (File Transfer Protocol) is a common method of uploading a Web site and related files to a Web server. Files can be uploaded via FTP in two different ways, and many software applica-tions allow you to transfer files to a Web server. Macromedia Dreamweaver, WS_FTP, and Claris Home page are just a few. Many schools already have software in place to handle file transfers. To use an FTP program, you will need to know to which directory on the Web server you will be sending your Web files. You will also need to know your assigned username and password (see Figure 9.5). Again, talk with your library media specialist or technology coordinator about which, if any, FTP software would be the best to use in your particular setting.

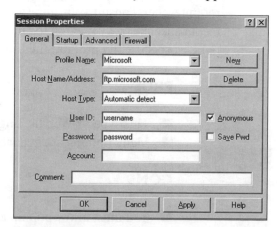

Figure 9.5: File Transfer Protocol (FTP)

Another way to send your files to a Web server via FTP is through your Web browser. Both Internet Explorer and Netscape Navigator support this file upload function. To use your Web browser to transfer files to the Web server, you will need to have a domain name and Web space already registered. Typically, you would use this option if you are utilizing a paid Web host. In the location bar at the top of your Web browser, type the following address: ftp://www.mywebsitename.com. Next, press the Enter or Return key. You will then be asked to enter a username and password. When you register with a paid Web host, you will choose a username and password. Enter this information when prompted. You will see all the folders located within your Web server directory. You should look for a folder labeled "WWW" or "public_html." Anything placed in this folder will be viewable online. Double click this folder. Once you open this folder, simply highlight the files you wish to upload to the server (i.e., index.html and index folder), and drag them to the WWW folder. You will probably see an upload progress bar. Once this progress bar disappears, your files are uploaded to the Web server and should be viewable online. If you have saved your Web site as "index.html," you can type your domain name into the location bar and view the Web site you have created.

HTTP

HTTP (Hypertext Transfer Protocol) is a method of uploading files through another Web page. Frequently, both free and paid Web hosts offer this service. When you are registering for a Web host, carefully read through the services offered to see whether files can be uploaded via HTTP or if a file upload center exists. A Web host that provides this service will have a Web page where you can browse for files on your own computer to upload to the Web server. Most Web hosts have directions for uploading files, as well as tech support to assist those who may be new to the procedure. Every Web host is slightly different, so make sure you thoroughly review the directions they provide.

For many, transferring files to a Web server is something rather foreign. Both FTP and HTTP are viable options for this particular task. Prior to publicizing your Web site, you should always attempt to view it online first to make sure it has been uploaded correctly. If you notice that pictures are missing or your Web site does not load properly when you type the domain name into the location bar, repeat the previous steps. Library media specialists can use their expertise to assist teachers with the file transfer process.

Library Media Connection

Library media specialists are instrumental in guiding classroom teachers through the process of publishing a Web site. If possible, collaborate with teachers and technology coordinators to offer professional development opportunities for faculty who are interested in uploading Web files to the school's Web server. Attempt to clearly define these procedures if they are not currently outlined in school district policy guides. You also can deliver workshops that focus on school Internet policy issues. As an experienced user of technology and Internet related applications, the library media specialist can contribute a great deal to this stage of the Web design process.

Mini Glossary

Directory A folder where Web files are stored.

FTP File Transfer Protocol—a method of uploading Web files to a server

HTTP Hypertext Transfer Protocol—a method of uploading files through another Web page

Upload Sending a Web site and related files to a Web server.

Web Browser or Browser A type of software, such as Internet Explorer or Netscape Navigator, which locates and displays a Web page.

Web Host A company or organization that provides the disk space for a Web site.

Web Server A computer that contains Web site files for display on the World Wide Web.

Chapter 10

Getting Noticed Worldwide

The world is so empty if one thinks only of mountains, rivers and cities; but to know someone here and there who thinks and feels with us, and though distant, is close to us in spirit—this makes the earth for us an inhabited garden.—Johann von Goethe

Now that you have successfully published your Web site, consider how people will find it. Of course your students will be able to find your Web site if you include your Web address (domain name) on assignments and project lists. You can draw global attention to your Web site in several different ways! Worldwide exposure provides many benefits. For example, your Web site can act as a conduit by which you can establish connections between your library or classroom and other libraries or classrooms internationally. You've put in the time, effort, and creativity necessary to design a Web site; why not let the whole world know about it?

Search Engine Submission

Search engines are powerful tools for locating resources online, tools that most people use when looking for a certain type of Web site. Basically, they search through a database of Web pages, looking for pages that match certain search criteria that have been entered. You will then be presented with a list of possible Web sites that contain the keywords specified. Consequently, if your Web site is not a part of a search engine's database, then it will not be listed in the search results.

So how does a Web site become a part of a search engine's database so that others are able to access it? If you visit a search engine such as Yahoo!, Google, Excite, Lycos, or MSN, you will most likely see a link that reads "Add URL" or "Submit a Site." If you click this link, you will be taken to a Web page that provides directions about adding a Web site to the search engine's database or directory. Take the time to read these directions because every search engine uses a slightly different procedure for adding Web sites to its database. Eventually, you will be taken to a feedback form that asks for your contact information, Web site name, and your Web address. You will also be asked to list keywords that are relevant to your Web site. Keywords are the words you want to be identified with your site. When you enter these words into a search engine, your Web site will then be listed in the results. For example, if you have created a Web site that focuses on the summer Olympic Games, you might want to enter the following keywords: Olympics, decathlon, track, field, swimming, diving, gold medal, and Olympian. Enter as many keywords as you are able. These keywords will usually be contained in the text of the Web site. This increases the chance that a user who has entered similar keywords will locate your Web site through a search engine. Once you have submitted the form, it will probably take between two weeks to a month for your Web site to become a part of the search engine's database. This is primarily due to the large volume of Web sites that are submitted daily to the major search engines.

Currently, a project is underway to create the largest Web directory in the world. It is known as the Open Directory Project and can be accessed by going to <www.dmoz.org>. If you submit your Web site to the Open Directory Project, it will be listed with literally hundreds of different search engines around the world. This can spare you from having to submit your Web site individually to each search engine. Fee-based search engine submission services will submit your Web site automatically to hundreds or even thousands of search engines worldwide. However, because so many free resources are available online, you may want to explore these possibilities before resorting to paying a fee for this service.

Link Trading

Another effective method of increasing your Web site's exposure is through something known as "link trading." Link trading essentially means that another Web site agrees to add a link to your Web site, and in exchange you agree to post a link to their site from yours. In this way, a new Web site developer can "draft off" the popularity of a better known Web site.

If you design a Web site about penguins and want to garner more attention for your site, you might begin by using a search engine to locate Web sites that are similar to yours. You would notice that when you searched for the keywords "penguin" and "Antarctica," a number of Web sites are listed. You would look to see which sites are the most popular. As you visit each of the top Web sites about penguins, you would check whether they contain a related links page. If they do, you would send an e-mail to the webmaster with your Web address, a short description of your Web site, and a request to add your Web site to the list of links. In return, you would state that you will add a link from your Web site to the other Web site. Most webmasters will agree to this arrangement, as they, too, wish to draw more visitors to their site.

Link trading is a win-win situation for everybody involved. The lesser-known Web site takes advantage of the daily traffic of a well-established Web site, while the well-established site continues to increase its visibility, as well as the variety of links it offers to its visitors. Whenever possible, endeavor to trade links with Web sites that address a topic similar to yours.

News Release

Newspapers, newsletters, and magazines reach thousands upon thousands of people on a daily basis. Why not take advantage of this traditional medium to promote your newly created Web site? Does your community have a newspaper that is looking for stories of local interest? If so, take a moment to send the editor a letter or e-mail describing how you enrich the learning experience through your Web site. Do you belong to a professional organization, such as the National Education Association or the American Association of School Librarians? Let them know about your Web site as well. If your school district has a public relations director, make sure to send this person information concerning the role your Web site plays in enhancing classroom instruction. Often, a public relations director has media contacts and can greatly facilitate the process of gaining publicity for your Web site. Be proud of the site you have developed. Let the world know about it!

Award Recognition

Many Web sites exist that deal primarily with bestowing recognition upon other Web sites for what they bring to the online community. These sites present awards to other Web sites for design, content, and more. To find award Web sites, use a search engine and the keywords "award, Web site, Web awards." If you decide that you would like to be nominated for such Web awards, simply send an e-mail to the site's webmaster, or fill out an online award recognition form. Include your Web address, the site description, and a brief explanation of why you believe your Web site deserves an award.

Once you have contacted the award Web site, you should receive a reply e-mail in a few weeks' time. Typically, the reviewers will use this time to evaluate your site and determine whether it is deserving of an award. Make sure that your site fits the award criteria specified on the site. For example, if your Web site discusses various types of poetry, do not submit it for a math award.

Award sites proudly display links to Web sites that have won their awards. This will draw further attention to your Web site and increase the number of daily visitors. Winning a Web award can also provide a good reason for requesting a news release, as previously discussed.

Library Media Connection

Library media specialists can provide direction to teachers who are seeking search engines and online directories to which they can submit their Web sites. Visit various search engines, and become familiar with their Web site submission policies. Develop a directory of academic Web sites divided into subject categories. Many of the webmasters of these Web sites will probably be interested in link trading in one form or another, especially with another Web site that is educationally oriented.

Mini Glossary

Keywords Words or phrases that are entered into a search field of a search engine to locate relevant Web sites.

Search Engine A tool on the Web that allows a user to search for Web sites based on certain criteria.

PART II

Student-Created Web Portfolios

You must be the change you wish to see in the world. —Mahatma Gandhi

Chapter 11

The Time for Web Portfolios Has Come

Blinded, you think only of home. You do not realize that it is the journey that makes up your life. — Homer, *The Odyssey*

Through his decade-long journey to find his way back to his beloved homeland, the Greek hero Odysseus learned that there was only one man who knew the way back to Ithaca, a blind prophet, who no longer dwelled in the land of the living. Determined to return to his wife and son, Odysseus travels to the underworld to seek an answer to his question. When confronted with this question, the prophet speaks to the deeper longing within Odysseus' heart. He observes, "Blinded, you think only of home. You do not realize that it is the journey itself that makes up your life."

As educators, we often find ourselves focusing a great deal of time and energy on the end result. Our world, it seems, is driven by the bottom line — the product. This emphasis on the outcome is undoubtedly important, but the journey, or process of learning, must not be neglected. The process must be understood, appreciated, and even celebrated. As Homer masterfully notes in his epic, life is lived in the journey!

What Is a Portfolio?

Imogene Forte and Sandra Schurr in *Making Portfolios, Products, and Performances Meaningful and Manageable for Students and Teachers*, propose that a portfolio is "… a well-planned and organized collection of artifacts or selected pieces of student work. When used collaboratively by the student and the teacher, portfolios can monitor and measure the growth of a student's knowledge, skills, and attitudes in a specific subject area" (11). In essence, a portfolio traces and describes a student's progress throughout the learning process. Portfolios can be specific to a certain subject area, or they can reflect interdisciplinary efforts. Portfolios traditionally have been a physical collection of student work, such as tests, essays, projects, or artwork, usually contained in folders or boxes.

What Is an Electronic Portfolio or "E-portfolio?"

An electronic portfolio, or "e-portfolio," is simply a meaningful collection of student work that has been created in an electronic format. Various software packages can be used to develop e-portfolios, such as Microsoft PowerPoint® or HyperStudio®. This book encourages the use of Microsoft PowerPoint due to its strong visual and interactive attributes.

What Is a Web Portfolio?

A Web portfolio is essentially an electronic portfolio that has been uploaded to a Web server so that it is viewable online. Examples of Web portfolios could include a student-created Web site, a PowerPoint Show, or a PowerPoint presentation that has been uploaded to a Web server. Web portfolios showcase student work globally, making it possible for educators, administrators, and parents to observe student growth over a period of time.

Why Incorporate Web Portfolios into the Learning Process?

The following are reasons why Web portfolios should be integrated into the learning process:

- The development of Web portfolios encourages students to take a more active role in their own learning. A Web portfolio focuses an individual student's interests and goals.
- Educators who have implemented Web portfolios into their curriculum have found that student motivation tends to increase. In fact, studies have demonstrated that students are motivated by activities that they consider "interactive, personally meaningful, and fun." (McCombs, 1991, 117–127; 1993, 287–313; 1994, 49–69). Web portfolios fit perfectly into these student-significant categories. Greg Hayward, a social studies teacher at Seneca Valley Middle School exclaims, "My students are excited! They can't wait to come in to class and start working on their Web portfolios!"
- Web portfolios are an excellent way to reach learners who have slipped through the cracks of our educational system. Web portfolios address the needs of visual, auditory, and kinesthetic learners through the use of images, video, sound, music, and the manipulation of graphics.
- Web portfolios allow educators to easily assess the level to which learning outcomes have been achieved.
- The examination of student Web portfolios provides educators with a valuable opportunity for self-reflection.
- Web portfolios are accessible. Parents, students, educators, and administrators can easily access a Web portfolio from any computer that has an Internet connection. As educators, we understand how crucial parental involvement is to education. A Web portfolio serves to further engage parents in the learning process by acting as a point of discussion concerning student progress.
- Web portfolios increase student interest through the use of multimedia, such as sound, animation, graphics, colors, and video.
- Web portfolios are easy for students to maintain and update. As students learn and process new information throughout the school year, they may wish to include additional showcase items, or "artifacts" (e.g., test scores, essays, and digital photos of projects). A Web portfolio is a work in progress that changes as a student learns and grows.
- Web portfolios, as well as other kinds of electronic portfolios, present few storage problems. They can be stored on a floppy disk, CD-R, computer hard drive, or a Web server.

Electronic Portfolios vs. Traditional Portfolios

For years, the development of portfolios has provided an excellent opportunity for students and educators to assess learning in a real and meaningful way. Student portfolios have traditionally been organized in a variety of ways, including file folders, shoe boxes, pizza boxes, or other containers. If the traditional portfolio process has been successful up to now, why attempt to adapt the portfolio process to an electronic format? The following chart will provide a rationale.

Issue	Traditional	Electronic (Web)
Motivation	Students tend to view traditional portfolios as merely a task that has to be performed. Storing and cataloging learning artifacts for the purposes of reflection is effective but does not usually inspire.	Electronic portfolios increase student motivation by allowing a student to easily display his work to others worldwide.
Accessibility	Traditional portfolios are difficult to showcase. Parents and administrators often will never see the results of a student's efforts.	Students are able to upload electronic portfolios to a Web sever, which permits parents and administrators to access the portfolio online.
Multimedia	Traditional portfolios typically do not contain multimedia. Exceptions may include an audiocassette of a student speech or videotape of a student performance.	Multimedia can be fully incorporated into an electronic portfolio, including sound, animation, graphics, and video.
Focus	The portfolio process is innately student-centered rather than teacher-centered.	The electronic portfolio process is student-centered and fosters active student learning to an even greater degree.
Presentation	Traditional portfolios are difficult to present due to size and organizational issues.	Electronic portfolios can be easily presented using a computer screen or an LCD projector. When uploaded to a server, Web portfolios can be presented to anybody in the world with an Internet connection.

Figure 11.1: Traditional Portfolios vs. Electronic Portfolios

By comparing and contrasting these two portfolio types, it becomes clear that electronic portfolios have certain advantages over the traditional portfolio system. From the use of multimedia to the increase in student motivation, the benefits of the electronic portfolio system are outstanding. So, indeed, the time for Web portfolios has come!

Library Media Connection

Library media specialists have a unique perspective, one not easily attained by the classroom teacher; they are able to gain a general overview of the teaching methods used in many different subject areas. This special insight into a variety of instructional techniques can be of great value to a classroom teacher who is attempting to integrate Web portfolios into the educational process. Often, library media specialists can help classroom teachers discover solutions that may be "outside the box," concerning Web portfolios, through the establishment of cross-curricular connections. Interdisciplinary Web portfolios can be developed that highlight student learning across the subject areas. As seasoned users of technology, they are able to assist in its application to the learning environment. When library media specialists collaborate with teachers, drawing upon their collective curricular and technological experience, the implementation of Web portfolios is greatly streamlined.

Involve school administration in the Web portfolio process whenever possible to encourage collaboration between classroom teachers and the school librarian. Studies have found that when principals expect teachers to work cooperatively with library media specialists, the effect on the learning process is extremely positive (van Deusen 17–25). As educators, we should attempt to tap those untapped resources.

Mini Glossary

Electronic Portfolio or E-Portfolio   A portfolio that has been created using an electronic format such as Microsoft PowerPoint.

PowerPoint Show   A type of file that automatically runs a Microsoft PowerPoint slide show. A student-created electronic portfolio can be saved as a PowerPoint Show and uploaded to a Web server.

Web Portfolio   A type of electronic or e-portfolio that can be viewed via the Internet.

Chapter 12

Web Portfolio Content

Know thyself. — Socrates

So, what should a Web portfolio include? A portfolio by definition is an organized and meaningful collection of a student's work. Remember that for students to feel a sense of ownership over a Web portfolio, they need to have decision-making power over what is included. Nonetheless, you should set guidelines within which students can operate. All Web portfolios should at least contain examples of the following:

- Artifacts — student work such as test/quiz scores, essays, projects, and reports
- Learning — student commentary, summarizing what was learned during a particular unit
- Reflection — student self-assessment, reflecting upon performance, personal goals, effort, learning strategies, and areas of improvement

Artifacts

As examples of real student work, artifacts do not necessarily need to represent the student's best academic performances. For instance, a student might select a poor test score for inclusion in his Web portfolio so that he will reflect upon what he will do to improve next time. A Web portfolio demonstrates learning, not just performance. Artifacts should be accompanied by a brief description of the assignment and the date on which it was given. Encourage students to think carefully about what artifacts they want to include in their Web portfolio. Artifacts might include the following:

Tests/Quizzes

Tests and quizzes are important means of assessment that students might want to include in their portfolio. How can a test or quiz be added to a Web portfolio? The most basic method of including an exam in a Web portfolio is simply to input the test scores into a PowerPoint slide, along with a title and description of the test. Another method would be to scan the student's actual test, converting it into a digital image that can be inserted into a PowerPoint slide.

Writing Samples

Writing samples (e.g., essays, journal responses, creative writing, poetry, and reports) often reflect student growth in a number of areas. Consequently, it is important to discuss ways in which they can be included in a Web portfolio. One suggestion is to have students use Microsoft Word® to complete their writing assignments. The Word documents would then be saved into the same folder that holds their Web portfolio (PowerPoint presentation). A hyperlink could be created in a PowerPoint slide to the Word document containing the students' writing samples. Another method is to digitally scan the writing samples and insert them as images into PowerPoint slides.

Projects

Projects that call for a student to construct, design, or devise something are an important part of the learning process, often requiring the student to utilize higher order thinking skills. Projects such as shadow boxes, wall maps, or models are great artifacts for students to include in their Web portfolio. Obviously, placing the project into an electronic format is impossible, but there is another way! A digital camera can be used to take photographs of the project from different angles. One or more digital photographs can be inserted into a PowerPoint slide to represent the entire project.

Video or Audio Clip of a Performance

A performance, such as a speech, skit, play, or debate, can be a benchmark event for students and something they would want to recognize in their Web portfolio. Performances can be included in two ways. First, a library media specialist or a teacher or another classmate can make a video recording of the performance using a digital video camera. The video can then be loaded on to a computer hard drive as a file. The file should be located in the same folder as the student's Web portfolio. Using a "Text & Media Clip" slide, the video can be inserted into a PowerPoint presentation. Audio clips can be captured with a computer microphone, a digital recording device, or a tape recorder. Most computers are outfitted with a microphone, so if you are using this method, the audio file will automatically be rendered in a digital format, ready to save into the student's Web portfolio folder. If you are using a digital recording device, you will need to load the file to the computer and save it into the Web portfolio folder. Finally, if you have a standard tape recording device, an easy way to convert the audio recording into a digital file is to play the recording next to the computer microphone, re-recording it digitally. Through a "Text & Media Clip" slide (refer to Chapter 4), the audio clip can be inserted into a PowerPoint presentation.

Graphs/Charts, Technical Drawings, Maps

Learning in the classroom is often assessed through the creation of graphs, charts, technical drawings, and maps. Students who are particularly proud of an assignment such as this would probably want to include it in their Web portfolio. If a chart or graph needs to be produced, a student could use a "Text & Chart" slide (refer to Chapter 4) to create it. This would be an easy way to incorporate this type of assignment into a Web portfolio. Maps and technical drawings can be scanned if they are the proper size, or the student can use a digital camera to take photographs of the assignment. These images can then be inserted into PowerPoint slides.

Learning

Learning happens throughout the days, weeks, months, and years of our lives. Most of us pay little or no attention to the process of learning itself, and therefore have no real understanding of how we learned what we did. Web portfolios challenge students to look back and evaluate what they have learned throughout the course of the school year. To initiate the learning portion of the Web portfolio process, have your students create a new slide following each artifact slide that encapsulates new information that was learned. You may want to have them use a bulleted list slide to write statements that summarize the content learned during the unit of instruction. This process of review is an excellent way to reinforce learning.

Images or multimedia files saved on disk or hard drive that relate to information learned can also be inserted into a PowerPoint slide. Graphics, photographs, and animated images can be harvested from a Web site and pasted into a slide (review chapters 7 and 8 for more information). For instance, a student who just completed a social studies unit focusing on ancient Egyptian civilization might add a digital photograph of the Great Pyramid of Khufu to the learning section of her Web portfolio.

Require students to reference the Web sites from which they borrow images. These references can be listed beneath each image or included in total on one final slide in the presentation, as a "Works Cited" slide. The ability to easily incorporate images and multimedia into the summary of the student learning section of a Web portfolio allows visual learners to express what they learned during a particular unit in a way that is meaningful and directly relates to their strengths.

Reflection

Web portfolios provide students with an opportunity to develop the positive habit of self-reflection, gaining a greater awareness of how they process and interpret information. Challenge your students to think carefully about why they chose the artifact they did. Students should insert a slide following each artifact slide with one to two paragraphs of reflection. You can have your students answer a series of questions about each artifact, questions that are designed to encourage reflective thinking. For example:

- Why did you choose to include this artifact in your Web portfolio?
- Were you pleased with your performance on this particular assignment? Why or why not?
- If you had the opportunity to do this assignment over, how would you do it differently?

Questions such as these impel students to employ higher order thinking skills. By evaluating their actions, performances, and assignments, students can gain valuable insights into their own work habits, interests, and learning styles. Aside from making the production of a Web portfolio more personally meaningful, the reflective process promotes the development of habits that will lead to future success.

Table of Contents

To make a Web portfolio more navigable, students should construct a table of contents. This should be the second slide in the presentation, just after the title slide. The table of contents should be the final item added to the Web portfolio, included only after the contents have been firmly established. PowerPoint makes this goal more attainable by automatically numbering each slide. To see the slide numbers, click "View," and drag down to "Slide Sorter" (see Figure 4.15, page 40). The table of contents gives the viewer,

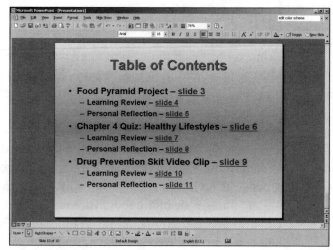

Figure 12.1: Table of Contents

whether parent, educator, administrator, or other student, a brief overview of the Web portfolio.

Each artifact title can be linked to its corresponding slide using the steps delineated in Chapter 7. In this way, a visitor can click on the assignment title and be taken directly to the slide that addresses that assignment. You may want to direct students to add a hyperlink to the table of contents slide from every slide in their presentation. This would allow a visitor to access the table of contents slide from any slide in the presentation, streamlining the navigation of the Web portfolio.

Library Media Connection

Create a Directory of Online Resources

The Web offers myriad resources for image and multimedia files. As mentioned, collaborate with teachers to develop a directory of Web sites and media files that students can utilize in the creation of their Web portfolios. Arrange the directory into topical categories to make the location of resources easy and efficient for students. This will also eliminate unnecessary student Web browsing.

Develop a Standardized Web Permission Form

Another issue that should be addressed by both library media specialists and teachers is the development of a Web portfolio permission form if one is not currently in use by the school district. Before students go online to search for images or media files to add to their Web portfolio, a parent or guardian should sign a statement permitting their child to access the Internet while at school. This form should be standardized and integrated into the Acceptable Use Policy. A Web portfolio permission form should require a parent or guardian to do the following:

■ Give the student permission to access the Internet.
■ Give the teacher permission to display student work online via a Web portfolio.

Mini Glossary

Artifacts Student work such as test/quiz scores, essays, projects, and reports.

Multimedia Refers to audio, video, animation, graphics, or a combination of each.

Presentation A group of PowerPoint slides arranged to present information.

Reflection Student self-assessment, reflecting upon performance, personal goals, effort, learning strategies, and areas of improvement.

Chapter 13

Tips for a Successful Experience in the Computer Lab

What one has not experienced, one will
never understand in print. —Isadora Duncan

If you are reading this chapter, hopefully you have already formed an idea of what you would like your students to include in their Web portfolios. We have discussed the benefits of implementing Web portfolios into the learning experience. Further, we have contemplated the specifics of what might be included in a Web portfolio. Now that it is time to put the Web portfolio process into practice, a number of issues must be considered. This chapter will offer suggestions for a successful experience in the computer lab.

Students and Computer Time

Allocating computers for the development of student Web portfolios can sometimes be a daunting task. In an ideal world, students would have access to their own computers, with unlimited time to creatively construct their Web portfolios. However, the reality we are faced with daily is that many schools experience shortages, especially in the area of technology. The key to this problem is making the best use of the resources your school has available. If fewer resources are accessible, then time management will be a challenge. The informational chart in Figure 13.1 on page 90 will suggest some ways in which to deal with obstacles to computer use.

Establishing Guidelines

Once you have made arrangements for your students to utilize the computer lab or library media center, you will want to consider establishing guidelines for the creation of Web portfolios. Clear guidelines are an important part of the Web portfolio process and will provide for a positive experience for students and educators. Figure 13.2 beginning on page 91 is an example of a guideline set that can be used in the computer lab.

Web portfolio guidelines clearly define what you would like your students to do. Additionally, this gives students a framework within which to work and be creative. Within the guidelines, they have the latitude to personalize their Web portfolio and make individual choices, such as which artifacts will be included in the Web portfolio, and which background colors, text sizes, and fonts to use.

Situation	Student-Computer Strategy	Time Management
School has a computer lab or library media center with 20–30 computer stations	Assign students to individual computer stations.	Schedule a block of time (2–3 days if possible) for students to develop Web portfolios. Make arrangements with other teachers to share computer time.
School has a computer lab, library media center, or mobile lap top station with 10–15 computer stations	Assign two students to each computer station.	Divide computer time so that each student has half of the period or block to develop their Web portfolio. Another option would be to have one student work all period, while the other writes learning summaries and reflections, or conducts research in the library. This often allows the second student to complete Web portfolio sections in less time. You could even have all of your students write the learning summary and reflective portions of the Web portfolio prior to actually using the computer.
School has a computer lab, library media center, or mobile lap top station with 10 or fewer computer stations	Have 10 or fewer students work on computers at a time.	This may require 3–4 days to complete. Have students work on an extended assignment that can be made up with relative ease. While a small group of students is working on Web portfolio development, have other students work on the assignment. Switch groups the next day and continue assignment.

Figure 13.1: Student to Computer Strategy and Time Management Establishing Guidelines

Sample Student Web Portfolio Guidelines

Phase	Tasks Assigned
1	■ Open the software. ■ Double click the Microsoft PowerPoint icon. ■ Choose "blank presentation."
2	■ Click the "Insert" menu and drag down to "New Slide." ■ Select the "Title slide" and click "OK." ■ In the text box that reads, "Click to add sub-title," click once and type your name.
3	■ Refer to the "Frequently Asked Questions" to change text size, color, font, slide background, or add an image. ■ Create 3 artifact slides. Click the "Insert" menu and drag down to "New Slide." ■ Select the "Bulleted List" slide and click "OK." ■ In the text box that reads "Click to add title," click once and type "Artifact." ■ You may choose from all tests, quizzes, projects, presentations, etc. ■ In the text box that reads "Click to add text," click once and type a brief description of the artifact, including the title and requirements. ■ Press the Enter or Return key to create another bullet. ■ Type your assessment results (i.e., test score). ■ Refer to the "Frequently Asked Questions" to change text size, color, font, slide background, or add an image, video, or audio file of the artifact.
4	■ Insert a learning slide after each artifact slide. ■ Click the "Insert" menu and drag down to "New Slide." ■ Select the "Bulleted List" slide and click "OK." ■ In the text box that reads "Click to add title," click once and type "Learning." ■ In the text box that reads "Click to add text," click once and type 1–2 paragraphs that summarize the new learning this artifact represents. ■ Refer to the "Frequently Asked Questions" to change text size, color, font, slide background, or to add an image.

Figure 13.2: Sample Student Web Portfolio Guidelines (page 1)

Sample Student Web Portfolio Guidelines (continued)

Phase	Tasks Assigned
5	■ Insert a reflection slide after each learning slide. ■ Click the "Insert" menu and drag down to "New Slide." ■ Select the bulleted list slide and click "OK." ■ In the text box that reads "Click to add title," click once and type "Reflection." ■ In the text box that reads "Click to add text," click once and type 1–2 paragraphs of personal reflection about the artifact you chose, by answering the following questions: • Why did you choose to include this artifact in your Web portfolio? • Were you pleased with your performance on this particular assignment? Why or why not? • If you had the opportunity to do this assignment over again, how would you do it differently? • Are there any other thoughts or feelings you would like to share about this particular artifact? ■ Refer to the "Frequently Asked Questions" to change text size, color, font, slide background, or add an image.
6	■ Go back and create a table of contents slide following your title slide. ■ Click the "Insert" menu and drag down to "New Slide." ■ Select the "Bulleted List" slide and click "OK." ■ In the text box that reads "Click to add title," click once and type "Table of Contents." ■ In the text box that reads "Click to add text," click once and type the title of the first artifact and the slide number. (To see the slide number, click on the "View" menu and drag down to "Slide Sorter.") ■ Refer to the "Frequently Asked Questions" to insert a hyperlink into this text. The hyperlink should connect the visitor to the slide that contains the artifact information. ■ Press the Enter or Return key to create another bullet. ■ Type the title of your second artifact and insert a hyperlink to the appropriate slide. ■ Repeat the steps for your third artifact. ■ Refer to the "Frequently Asked Questions" to change text size, color, font, slide background, or add an image.

Figure 13.2: Sample Student Web Portfolio Guidelines (page 2)

FAQ Sheets

A FAQ (Frequently Asked Questions) sheet is a list of commonly asked questions about Microsoft PowerPoint. It is designed to highlight the basic features of the software, discussed in detail in Chapters 4–10, in a simple outline form. It is advisable for library media specialists and teachers to provide this information to students prior to their arrival in the computer lab or library media center. A FAQ sheet encourages students to become self-sufficient learners by conditioning them to search out answers to their questions on their own. Creating a FAQ sheet can reduce the number of student questions directed to you. An example of a FAQ sheet begins on page 95 (Figure 13.4).

By providing a FAQ sheet, your role in the computer lab or library media center will become proactive rather than reactive.

Regularly Scheduled Updates to Web Portfolios

Students should have access to the computer lab or library media center on a monthly basis so that they can update their Web portfolios. For a Web portfolio to remain relevant, new artifacts, learning summaries, and personal reflections must be added regularly. Some educators might object, saying that instructional time would be sacrificed if students were permitted time to update their Web portfolios monthly. However, if Web portfolios are fully integrated into the educational structure, learning will be significantly enhanced through learning, review, reflection, student accountability, and higher order thinking.

Converting a PowerPoint Presentation to a Web Portfolio

Before students can present their final product, the PowerPoint presentation that they have been developing must be converted to a format suitable for online viewing. The following are a few possibilities to explore:

HTML Web Portfolio
As explained earlier, a PowerPoint presentation can be saved as a Web site. To accomplish this task, the steps that are outlined in Chapter 9 would be followed with your students (refer also to Figure 13.4: Frequently Asked Questions). Once the presentation has been successfully saved as a Web site, upload the files to a Web server via FTP or HTTP, as discussed in Chapter 9.

PowerPoint Show Web Portfolio
Another fairly simple solution for the conversion of a PowerPoint presentation to a Web portfolio is known as a PowerPoint Show. This option allows a visitor to view the student's Web portfolio as a slide show rather than a Web site. Once the student has completed the PowerPoint presentation, click on the "File" menu, and drag down to "Save As." You will see a new window appear, as in Figure 13.3.

Next to "Save File as Type:" select the "PowerPoint Show" option from the bar menu.

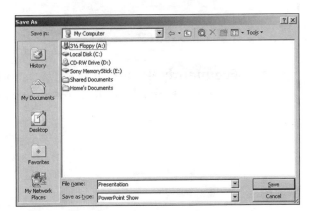

Figure 13.3: Saving a Presentation as a PowerPoint Show

Below "Save As:" type the name of the student's Web portfolio. To avoid confusion, it is recommended that the students' initials or last name be used as the file name. Choose the correct folder or directory in which to save the new file by clicking the selection bar at the top of the window and dragging down to the folder of choice. Once you have selected the appropriate folder, click "Save." The PowerPoint Show will now be located in the folder you have chosen. This file can be uploaded to a Web server by following the FTP or HTTP directions discussed in Chapter 9. When a visitor clicks on a hyperlink that is connected to this new PowerPoint Show file, the slide show will run automatically, displaying the Web portfolio.

PowerPoint Presentation

A PowerPoint presentation itself can be uploaded to a Web server and viewed online. Simply have the students save their presentation as they normally would. Make sure the file name of their presentation is their initials, last name, or another identifying name. Next, upload the presentation file to a Web server via FTP or HTTP, as discussed in Chapter 9. When a visitor accesses this file through a Web browser, the presentation will appear in the browser window itself. The visitor can then scroll down through a Web browser window to see each slide in the Web portfolio.

Library Media Connection

In the beginning of the school year, library media specialists and teachers should meet to discuss the various ability levels of the students who will be involved in the Web portfolio process. Think about ways in which student Web portfolio guidelines can be modified to fit the particular needs of the students. This will create a smoothly functioning environment in the library media center or computer lab.

Collaborate with teachers and administrators to establish guidelines for the library media center or computer lab with respect to scheduling computer time. Ask teachers to schedule computer time well in advance to avoid conflicts. Consult with teachers who may never have taken their students to the computer lab or library media center, and be available to assist students who are developing Web portfolios. Library media specialists are experienced users of technology; their direct involvement in the Web portfolio process is crucial for success.

Mini Glossary

Frequently Asked Questions or FAQ A list of questions that are commonly asked by students, along with their respective answers.

Web Portfolio FAQ Sheet

How do I insert a new slide into my presentation?
- Click "Insert" and drag down to "New Slide."
- Select from the options available.

How do I change text size and color?
- With your mouse cursor, highlight the text you want to change.
- Click the "Format" menu and drag down to "Font." A window will pop up, allowing you to change the "Font," the "Font Style," and the "Size." You may also change the "Effects" and the "Color."
- Make any changes and click "OK." You will see that your text has been changed.

How do I insert a hyperlink?
- Highlight the text in which you would like to insert a hyperlink, or click once on an image.
- Click the "Insert" menu and drag down to "Hyperlink."
- Below "Link to File or URL," type the URL to which you wish to link.
- If you would like to link to a file (i.e. a student essay in Microsoft Word or a video clip) click the "Select" button and search for the file on your computer.
- Once you are ready, click "OK" to insert the hyperlink.
- You should notice that the text has changed color if you inserted the hyperlink into text.

How do I change the background?
- Click the "Format" menu and drag down to "Background."
- Click the menu bar that shows the current background color. You may select a new color.
- If you would like to choose from more colors, click "More Colors."
- If you would like to add some fancy background effects, click "Fill Effects." You will see these last two choices when you click on the menu bar that shows the current background color. If you click on either of these last two choices, a new box will appear with some folder tabs at the top. You will first see the folder tab that says "Gradient." Experiment with "One Color," "Two Colors," and "Preset." Then try the "Texture" tab or "Pattern."
- When you are satisfied, click "OK" to see the changes.
- Then click "Apply" to apply this background to the slide, or "Apply to All" to apply the background to all of your slides.

How do I see the slides that I was working on previously?
- Use the Right-hand scroll bar to scroll through the slides you have already made.

How do I see all of my slides at once?
- Click the "View" menu and drag down to "Slide Sorter."
- If you want to delete a slide, simply click on it once and press the "Delete" or "Backspace" key.
- If you want to move a slide to a new position, click and drag it to a new position.

Figure 13.4: Web Portfolio FAQ Sheet (page 1)

Web Portfolio FAQ Sheet (continued)

How do I save my presentation?
- Click the "File" menu and drag down to "Save."
- Select the proper folder or directory where you would like to save your portfolio.
- Save your portfolio as your last name.
- Now every time you save your portfolio, the file will automatically go into the correct folder.

How can I add an image from the Internet to a slide?
- Open Microsoft Internet Explorer.
- When the Web browser opens, type the URL for the Web site you want to visit in the location bar.
- When you find a picture you would like to add to your slide, mouse over the image.
- Click and hold if you are using a Mac. Right click if you are using a PC. When the menu pops up, drag to "Copy Image," or "Copy."
- Click your PowerPoint slide to bring it to the front. Click the "Edit" menu and drag down to "Paste." The image should now appear on your slide.
- You can click the image and move it to any part of your slide.
- If the image covers text or another image, you can send it back one layer by right clicking the image if you are using a PC, or by clicking and pressing the "CTRL" key at the same time. A menu will appear. Drag down to "Arrange" or "Order" and drag across to "Send Backward." The image should move back one layer. Repeat if necessary.

How do I change the size of an image?
- Click the image once.
- Sizing handles should appear on the image. Click the corner handles and drag. The image will increase or decrease in size depending upon which way the sizing handles are dragged.

How do I add animation to my text or images?
- Click the text box or image that you would like to animate.
- Click the "Slide Show" menu, and drag down to "Preset Animation" or "Animation Scheme." Select the animation type from the menu.
- To view your animation, click the "View" menu and drag down to "Slide Show." Click to see your animation in action!

How do I change slide transition effects?
- Click the "Slide Show" menu and drag down to "Slide Transition."
- When the new window pops up, click the menu bar that is currently labeled "No Transition" and select a transition.
- If you would like to add a sound to your slide transition, select from the "Sounds" bar.
- Click "Apply" to add the transition to your slide. Click "Apply to All" if you want all of your slides to have the same effect.

Figure 13.4: Web Portfolio FAQ Sheet (page 2)

Web Portfolio FAQ Sheet (continued)

How do I create WordArt titles?

- Click the "Insert" menu and drag down to "Picture." Drag across to "WordArt."
- Select a style.
- When the text menu pops up, type your text and select a font and size.
- Click "OK" when you are finished.
- You may move your new title around the slide by clicking on it once and dragging it to a new position. See *How do I add animation?* and *How do I change the size of an image?*

How do I convert my PowerPoint presentation into an HTML Web Portfolio?

- Different versions of PowerPoint handle this action in different ways, but most will guide you through the process.
- Go to "File" and drag down to "Save as HTML" if you are using a Mac or next to "Save as type:" select "Web Page" if you are using a PC.
- Follow the directions provided if you are using a Mac or name your file and click "Save" if you are using a PC.
- Inform your teacher or library media specialist that you are ready to upload your files to the Web server.

How do I save my file as a PowerPoint Show Web Portfolio?

- Go to "File" and drag down to "Save As."
- From the options menu bars, select "Power Point Show."
- Name your file and click "Save."
- Inform your teacher or library media specialist that you are ready to upload your file to the Web server.

Figure 13.4: Web Portfolio FAQ Sheet (page 3)

Chapter 14

Student Presentation of Web Portfolios

Esse quam videri
To be, rather than appear.

When you create something that makes you proud, you want to let the whole world know about it. Your students are no different. You will probably observe that they put a great deal of effort and creative thought into their Web portfolios. The next step is to provide an opportunity for your students to present their Web portfolios.

Before the presentations begin, there are several factors to consider. Hellen C. Barrett, Ph.D., of the University of Alaska, Anchorage, advises in her article *Collaborative Planning for Electronic Portfolios: Asking Strategic Questions*, posted on the University of Alaska Anchorage Web site, that it is important to examine individual portfolio content to establish what material is audience appropriate and have the students modify presentations as appropriate (par. 12). She also advises educators to evaluate student presentations of Web portfolios. The following are suggested methods for presenting student Web portfolios. You might choose to use one or a combination.

Methods of Presenting a Web Portfolio

Classroom Presentation

Using an LCD projector and a projection screen or a SMART Board, students can present their Web portfolio to the entire class. Student portfolios can be assessed using a rubric as they are being presented. Students can field questions from you and from their fellow students regarding the artifacts, learning, or personal reflection included in their Web portfolio. If you choose this manner of presentation, you should remind students early on to select assignments and exam scores that they would not mind sharing with others, or else provide an opportunity for students to modify their Web portfolios prior to presentation.

This method of presentation can take time, due to the number of students that need to present to the class. You may want to limit student portfolio presentations to five minutes or less. Additionally, you should consider placing students into an order so that they will know exactly when they are to be ready to present. With a little organization, you can streamline this process so students have the opportunity to share their Web portfolios without compromising instructional time.

Parent-Educator-Student Presentation

Often, parents can feel out of touch with what their child is learning and doing at school. Student Web portfolios can be presented in a small group comprised of the student, the student's parents or guardian, and you, the educator. Parents and educators then have the opportunity to ask questions of the student. Smaller presentation groups can be scheduled at times and locations that are acceptable to all parties involved either at the end of the school year or throughout the year as a demonstration of work-in-progress. This presentation method has been shown to stimulate parental involvement in the learning process (Donati and Stefanacci, par. 1).

Online Presentation

A Web portfolio presentation can be integrated into an educator-created Web site. Using a "Bulleted List" slide (refer to Chapter 4), create a slide that contains links to student Web portfolios that are in HTML, PowerPoint Show, or PowerPoint Presentation format. Figure 14.1 shows what a student Web portfolios page might look like within the context of an educator-created Web site.

A link to your e-mail address can also be added to this Web page so that parents and administrators

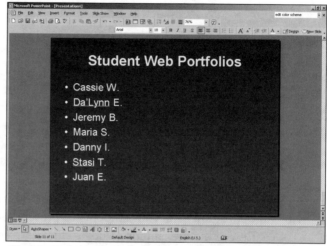

Figure 14.1: Online Presentation Web Page

can send comments after reviewing student Web portfolios. This method of presentation allows educators, parents, and administrators to confer electronically concerning student progress rather than attempting to organize a meeting around several busy schedules.

Assessment

Whenever an educator gives a student an assignment, student performance should always be assessed. This feedback is valuable for both students and educators. Did the student successfully meet the learning objectives? Did you as the educator successfully teach the material? Is some sort of additional review necessary? Do the items included in a Web portfolio demonstrate that the project has met national, state, or local standards? Web portfolios, like any other assignment, should be properly evaluated. How can a Web portfolio be adequately assessed when it is a collection of student artifacts, or assignments? You will need to decide which aspects of the project will be assessed. Are you going to evaluate spelling, grammar, content, design/layout, the use of multimedia, or a combination of several categories? Many educators have found that a rubric similar to Figure 14.2 is helpful.

Student presentation of Web portfolios provides an excellent opportunity for assessment. This allows students to share their creation, while at the same time you can evaluate their portfolio. When setting learner goals for Web portfolios, consider national, state, and local standards for your discipline. Library media specialists and teachers should collaborate to establish rubrics that authentically assess learning objectives. Rubric assessments should be clear, provide effective feedback, and be relatively easy to use. Their use in the assessment of Web portfolios is strongly encouraged.

Skill	Exceptional 5	Effective 4	Acceptable 3	Unsatisfactory 1
Multimedia Use				
Content				
Organization				
Learning Summaries				
Personal Reflection				
CATEGORY TOTALS				SCORE: ___/25

Figure 14.2: Web Portfolio Rubric

Library Media Connection

Library media specialists can facilitate Web portfolio presentations by providing professional development opportunities for teachers who may be unfamiliar with instructional technology such as LCD projectors or SMART Boards. If faculty members are trained early in the year, the presentation of student Web portfolios will be much more streamlined. The American Library Association (ALA) <www.ala.org> suggests that technology should be gradually integrated into traditionally taught courses (Information Literacy Competency Standards and Student Learning Outcomes). This would encompass any technologies that can be used for student Web portfolio presentations.

ALA further advises that a partnership should be formed between teachers and library media specialists to identify appropriate curriculum objectives and methods of assessment, taking into consideration students' age, abilities, and learning levels. This is especially important to the establishment of Web portfolio objectives. Prior to the implementation of Web portfolios, librarians and classroom teachers should collaborate to develop a rubric that assesses the goals and objectives.

Mini Glossary

LCD Projector A digital projector that can project the computer screen onto a much larger projection screen.

SMART Board A projection screen that allows a presenter to manipulate computer icons by touching the screen itself rather than using a mouse pointer.

Glossary

Artifacts Student work such as test/quiz scores, essays, projects, and reports.

Byte A unit of storage on a computer. A byte is 8 bits of data. A kilobyte is roughly 1,000 bytes, a megabyte is 1,000 kilobytes, and a gigabyte is 1,000 megabytes.

Directory A folder where Web files are stored.

Electronic Portfolio or E-Portfolio A student portfolio that has been created using an electronic format such as Microsoft PowerPoint.

E-Mail A message sent to a person or group electronically through the Internet.

Font An assortment of characters all of one style.

Frequently Asked Questions or FAQ A list of questions that are commonly asked by students, along with their respective answers.

FTP File Transfer Protocol—a method of uploading Web files to a server.

Hard Drive The device a computer uses to permanently store information or data.

Hardware The physical parts of a computer that can be touched, such as the screen and keyboard.

Home Page The first Web page of a Web site that a visitor will see—usually the most important page.

HTML Hypertext Markup Language—a programming language used for creating Web pages.

HTTP Hypertext Transfer Protocol—a method of uploading files through another Web page.

Hyperlink or Link A means of connecting one Web page with another, so that when selected, the related Web page will appear.

Internet A worldwide network connecting millions of computers for communications purposes.

Keywords	Words or phrases that are entered into a search field of a search engine to locate relevant Web sites.
LCD Projector	A digital projector that can project the computer screen onto a much larger projection screen.
Megahertz	A unit that measures the speed of a processor.
Multimedia	Refers to audio, video, animation, graphics, or a combination of these.
Operating System (OS)	The software on your computer that controls its basic functioning.
Portfolio	A collection of a student's work and learning experiences for the purposes of reflection and assessment.
PowerPoint Show	A type of file that automatically runs a Microsoft PowerPoint slide show. A student-created electronic portfolio can be saved as a PowerPoint Show and uploaded to a Web server.
Presentation	A group of PowerPoint slides arranged to present information.
Processor	The "brain" of the computer. A device that determines how quickly a computer can process information or data.
RAM	Random Access Memory. The memory available to run programs on a computer.
Reflection	Student self-assessment, reflecting upon performance, personal goals, effort, learning strategies, and areas of improvement.
Search Engine	A tool on the Web that allows a user to search for Web sites based on certain criteria.
Sizing Handles	The tiny squares that appear on each corner and each side of an image when the user clicks on it once. The sizing handles allow a user to adjust image size.
Slide	A basic part of a PowerPoint presentation.
Slide Transition	The movement from one PowerPoint slide to the next.
SMART Board	A projection screen that allows a presenter to manipulate computer icons by touching the screen itself rather than using a mouse pointer.
Software	An application or set of instructions that tells a computer what to do, usually intangible.

Text	The words, characters, and numbers utilized in a Web page.
Text Box	A rectangular area of a PowerPoint slide that contains text.
Upload	Sending a Web site and related files to a Web server.
URL	Uniform Resource Locator. A technical term for a Web address or domain name.
Web Browser or Browser	A type of software, such as Internet Explorer or Netscape Navigator, that locates and displays a Web page.
Web Editor	A type of software used for designing and editing Web pages.
Web Host	A company or organization that provides the disk space for a Web site.
Webmaster	The person who manages a Web site; the administrative contact.
Web Page or Web Site	A document or group of electronic documents that can be accessed through the Internet.
Web Portfolio	A type of electronic or e-portfolio that can be viewed via the Internet.
Web Server	A computer that contains Web site files for display on the World Wide Web.
Window	Rectangular portion of a display being used by a specific program.
World Wide Web or WWW or Web	An interface for the Internet, made up of computers that provide access to documents that further provide access to other documents, multimedia files, and Web pages.

Bibliography

Baker, Eva L. "Technology: How Do We Know It Works?" U.S. Department of Education. 1999.
    <http://www.ed.gov/Technology/TechConf/1999/whitepapers/paper5.html>.

Barrett, Helen C. "Collaborative Planning for Electronic Portfolios: Asking Strategic Questions." University of
    Alaska, Anchorage. 1997. <http://transition.alaska.edu/www/portfolios/planning.html>.

Chaney, Bradford. *School Library Media Centers: 1993–94*. Washington, DC: U.S. Department of Education.
    National Center for Education Statistics. 1998.

Clarke, Arthur C. *Profiles of the Future: An Inquiry into the Limits of the Possible*. London: Gollancz Ltd. 1999.

Donati, Thomas & Leo Stefanacci. "Student Conferences." Seneca Valley Middle School. 2003.
    <http://www.seneca.k12.pa.us/~donatit/studentconferences.htm>.

Forte, Imogene & Sandra Schurr. *Making portfolios, products, and performances meaningful and manageable for
    students and teachers*. Nashville, Tenn.: Incentive Publications, Inc. 1995.

"Guidance on the Enhancing Education Through Technology (Ed Tech) Program." U.S. Department of Education.
    2002. <http://www.ed.gov/offices/OESE/esea/edtechguidance.doc>.

Hayward, Greg. Personal interview. 28 Feb. 2003.

"Information Power: Building Partnerships for Learning." American Library Association and Association for
    Educational Communications and Technology. 1998. <http://www.ala.org/aasl/ip_principles1.html>.

"Information Literacy Competency Standards and Student Learning Outcomes." American Library Association.
    2002.
    <http://www.ala.org/Content/NavigationMenu/ACRL/Issues_and_Advocacy1/
    Information_Literacy1/ACRL_Information_Literacy_Web_Site/
    Standards_Toolkit/Using_the_Standards/standardsintro.ppt>.

Johnston, P. & R.L. Allington, "Remediation." In R. Barr, M. L. Kamil, P. Mosenthal, & P. D. Pearson (Eds.),
    Handbook of Reading Research. 1991. Vol. II, 984–1012.

Ladd, E. David. "Enhancing the Learning Process with PowerPoint." *Teaching Matters: Office for Teaching and
    Learning Newsletter*, April 2001, Volume 5, No.8: 2.

Loschert, Kristin. "Are You Ready?" *NEA Today*, April 2003, Volume 21, No.7: 9.

McCombs, B.L. "Learner-Centered Psychological Principles for Enhancing Education: Applications in School
    Settings." *The Challenges in Mathematics and Science Education: Psychology's Response*. 1993:
    287–313.

McCombs, B.L. "Motivation and Lifelong Learning." *Educational Psychologist*, 1991: 26(2), 117–127.

McCombs, B. L. "Strategies for Assessing and Enhancing Motivation: Keys to Promoting Self-Regulated
    Learning and Performance." *Motivation: Theory and Research*. 1994: 49–69.

Means, Barbara. "Congressional Web-Based Education Commission Hearing." SRI International. 2000.
    < http://www.sri.com/news/releases/04-07-00.html>.

Mustapha, Ramlee. "Diverse Learners in Vocational and Technical Education: Strategies for Success." 2000.
    <http://digest.myvirtec.net/pdf/Ramlee2.pdf>.

Niguidula, D. "Picturing performance with digital portfolios." *Educational Leadership*. 1997: 55(3), 26–29.

Van Deusen, J.D. & J.L. Tallman, "The Impact of Scheduling on Curriculum Consultation and Information Skills
    Instruction: Part One: The 1993–94 AALS/Highsmith Research Award Study." *School Library Media
    Quarterly*. 1994: 23 (1), 17–25.

"What's a WebQuest." San Diego State University. 1995. <http://webquest.sdsu.edu/overview.htm>.

Zernike, Kate. "The Feng Shui of Schools." *New York Times*. Late Edition, section 4A: 20. 23 May 2003.
    <http://query.nytimes.com/gst/abstract.html?res=F30B10F83E590C768CDDA10894D9404482>.

Index